DR. ACKERMAN'S BOOK OF BOXERS

LOWELL ACKERMAN DVM

BB-105

Overleaf: The Boxer has it all — elegance, stature, and power! This handsome brindle male represents just one of the hundreds of Jacquet Boxer champions bred by America's premier breeder Richard Tomita.

The author has exerted every effort to ensure that medical information mentioned in this book is in accord with current recommendations and practice at the time of publication. However, in view of the ongoing advances in veterinary medicine, the reader is urged to consult with his veterinarian regarding individual health issues.

Photography by: Edward Berkeley, Elizabeth DeGroff, Christine Filler, Isabelle Francais, Dr. Kenneth Jeffery, Jean Loney, Dorrell-Jo MacWhinnie, Linda Michaels, Josie O'Reilly, Tom O'Reilly, Vince Serbin, Wendy Wallner.

The presentation of pet products in this book is strictly for instructive purposes only; it does not constitute an endorsement by the author, publisher, owners of dogs portrayed, or any other contributors.

Distributed in the UNITED STATES to the Pet Trade by T.F.H. Publications, Inc., One T.F.H. Plaza, Neptune City, NJ 07753; distributed in the UNITED STATES to the Bookstore and Library Trade by National Book Network, Inc. 4720 Boston Way, Lanham MD 20706; in CANADA to the Pet Trade by H & L Pet Supplies Inc., 27 Kingston Crescent, Kitchener, Ontario N2B 2T6; Rolf C. Hagen Inc., 3225 Sartelon St. Laurent-Montreal Quebec H4R 1E8; in CANADA to the Book Trade by Vanwell Publishing Ltd., 1 Northrup Crescent, St. Catharines, Ontario L2M 6P5 ; in ENGLAND by T.F.H. Publications, PO Box 15, Waterlooville PO7 6BQ; in AUSTRALIA AND THE SOUTH PACIFIC by T.F.H. (Australia), Pty. Ltd., Box 149, Brookvale 2100 N.S.W., Australia; in NEW ZEALAND by Brooklands Aquarium Ltd. 5 McGiven Drive, New Plymouth, RD1 New Zealand; in Japan by T.F.H. Publications, Japan—Jiro Tsuda, 10-12-3 Ohjidai, Sakura, Chiba 285, Japan; in SOUTH AFRICA by Lopis (Pty) Ltd., P.O. Box 39127, Booysens, 2016, Johannesburg, South Africa. Published by T.F.H. Publications, Inc.
MANUFACTURED IN THE
UNITED STATES OF AMERICA
BY T.F.H. PUBLICATIONS, INC.

CONTENTS

DEDICATION

To my wonderful wife Susan and my three adorable children, Nadia, Rebecca and David.

PREFACE

Keeping your Boxer healthy is the most important job that you, as an owner, can do. Whereas there are many books available that deal with breed qualities, conformation and show characteristics, this may be the only book available dedicated entirely to the preventative health care of the Boxer. This information has been compiled from a variety of sources and assembled here to provide you with the most up-to-date advice available.

This book will take you through the important stages of selecting your pet, screening it for inherited medical and behavioral problems, meeting its nutritional needs, and seeing that it receives optimal medical care.

So, enjoy the book and use the information to keep your Boxer the healthiest it can be for a long, full and rich life.

Lowell Ackerman DVM

BIOGRAPHY

D r. Lowell Ackerman is a world-renowned veterinary clinician, author, lecturer and radio personality. He is a Diplomate of the American College of Veterinary Dermatology and is a consultant in the fields of dermatology, nutrition and genetics. Dr. Ackerman is the author of 34 books and over 150 book chapters and articles. He also hosts a national radio show on pet health care and moderates a site on the World Wide Web dedicated to pet health care issues (http://www.familyinternet.com/pet/pet-vet.htm).

BREED HISTORY

THE GENESIS OF THE MODERN BOXER

The Boxer descended from the mastiff family of dogs that was believed to have originated in Asia. These dogs were prized for their courage and were used as guard dogs, hunting dogs and for fighting. Some breed enthusiasts claim that early drawings of the breed show they were present in Egypt and Greece but most believe it is impossible to substantiate those claims.

Facing page: Today's Boxer is an elegant working dog — far more stylish and impressive than his molossus forebears. Owned by Pat Mullen.

The mastiff-type dogs eventually were widely disseminated all across Europe.

In all likelihood, it was the Romans who helped perpetuate the breed now known as the Boxer. It was believed that the Romans imported British Mastiffs known as *Bullenbeissers* (bull-biter) and bred them to the Molossus breed to yield German Bullenbeissers. The Danzinger Bullenbeisser was used for hunting deer, bear and wild pigs and a smaller version, the Brabanter Bullenbeisser, was the direct ancestor to the Boxer.

The Brabanter was crossed with other dogs such as the Great Dane and the English Bulldog and selectively bred to achieve a smaller size than the Mastiff.

The Great Dane is part of the Boxer's origin—he was crossed with the Brabanter Bullenbeisser, a now-extinct German dog that is known to be one of the Boxer's direct ancestors. Owned by Lois Ostrowski.

The Brabanter was crossed with the English Bulldog in order to produce a dog that was smaller than the Brabanter's Mastiff predecessors.

The Brabanter eventually became extinct, but its descendant, the "Boxl," was a guard dog to the butcher and slaughterer. Its common appeal earned it several derisive nicknames, including "herding mutt" and "knife grinder." It is hypothesized that the Bull Terrier and Giant Schnauzer were also incorporated into the breed soon to be known as Boxer.

In 1894, Friedrich Roberth wrote a detailed account of the breed and was the first to use the name "Boxer." Until then, the breed was not given its due respect. However, after that, things changed. The Boxer Club was officially formed in 1895 and, in 1904, the first Boxer was registered in the American Kennel Club Stud Book. In World War I, the Boxer was used as a pack animal, a scout, a messenger and even as a mail dog. The breed was still slow to gain in popularity and, by 1930, there were still less than 20 Boxers in the country. However, in 1994, the Boxer was the 15th most commonly registered breed with the American Kennel Club.

MIND & BODY

**PHYSICAL AND BEHAVIORAL TRAITS
OF THE BOXER**

I f you're looking for a dog with style to spare, look no further than the Boxer. He's got it. And along with style he's got smarts. Put the two together  and you've got a canine companion who's eager to please, knows what he's do-ing, and whose beauty impresses all who meet him.

Facing page: The Boxer is capable of being an impressive presence in the show ring as well as a loyal and loving family pet. This fawn Boxer is owned by Rick Tomita.

CONFORMATION AND PHYSICAL CHARACTERISTICS

This is not a book about show dogs, so information here will not deal with the conformation of champions and how to select one. The purpose of this chapter is to provide basic information

The Boxer was originally bred to have a protruding lower jaw for increased leverage and holding power, thus creating a dog with a naturally undershot bite.

about the stature of a Boxer and qualities of a physical nature.

Clearly, beauty is in the eye of the beholder. And, since standards come and standards go, measuring your dog against some imaginary yardstick does little for you or your dog. Just because your dog isn't a show champion doesn't mean that he or she is any less of a family member. And, just because a dog is a champion doesn't mean that he or she is not a genetic time bomb waiting to go off.

When breeders and those interested in showing Boxers are selecting dogs, they are looking for those qualities that match the breed "standard." This standard, however, is of an imaginary Boxer and it changes from time to time and from country to country. Thus, the conformation and physical characteristics that pet owners should concentrate on are somewhat different and much more practical.

Boxers were originally bred to be medium sized dogs but, as they were used for more and more guard work, they were bred to become progressively larger. Most adult males are 22–24 inches at the withers and bitches are about 1 inch smaller. The normal weight range for the breed is 55–70 pounds but a better target is about 60 pounds for females and 65 pounds for males. Larger dogs are not necessarily better dogs. Boxers were never intended to be considered "giants" and the increased size might promote some medical problems that tend to be more common in larger dogs. There is some preliminary evidence that the larger members of the breed might not only be more susceptible to orthopedic disorders such as elbow dysplasia and hip dysplasia, but also to heart ailments such as dilated cardiomyopathy. DNA testing is currently being researched and should help answer these and other questions related to size and genetic passage of medical problems.

The original Boxers were agile and powerful and had short deep muzzles and a protruding lower jaw, which gave them leverage and allowed them to hold their quarry longer. This created an irregular "bite" in the breed. Boxers have an undershot jaw but poor breeding practices can create a dog with real dental problems.

Boxer puppies have floppy ears and lovely tails unless there is surgical intervention. Be aware that it is not necessary to either crop ears or dock tails in the Boxer for it to be a purebred. Being a true Boxer has to do with genetics, not surgery. For

The normal size of a male Boxer is between 22–24 inches at the withers; bitches are about an inch smaller. The normal weight range is between 55–70 pounds, with 65 pounds for males and 60 pounds for females being the "target" weights.

those wanting to indulge, tails and dewclaws tend to be docked when pups are 3 days old; ears are most often cropped at about 6–8 weeks of age. Most veterinary associations and even many breed registries are against altering animals to create an artificial image. Consider carefully your rationale if you decide to have these procedures done.

COAT COLOR, CARE AND CONDITION

There are only two acceptable colors in the Boxer: fawn and brindle and both may have some white marking (flash). The brindling gene (E^{br}) is dominant such that breeding two brindle Boxers yields predominantly brindles. Since fawn is recessive to brindle, breeding two fawns produces only fawns. Breeding fawn to brindle produces both fawn and brindle.

All Boxers have short coats and are easy to groom. They should be brushed 2–3 times a week and this helps remove dead fur and fleas and adds sheen to the coat. Boxers are moderate

Julia's Willie, owned by Dorrell-Jo MacWhinnie, shows the striking black and orange coloration of a brindle coat.

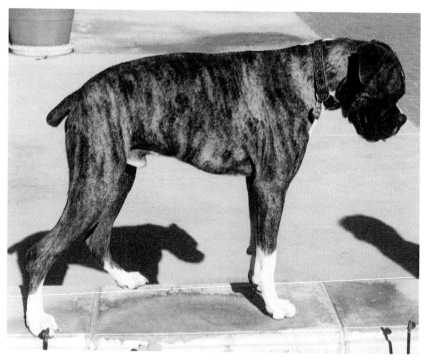

Fawn is an acceptable coat color for the Boxer. Atocha's Ms. Em-Erika, known as "Emma," takes a break after a romp in the grass.

shedders but they also tend to groom themselves (like a cat) and keep themselves quite clean. A bath is needed every month or so depending on the individual situation. A moisturizing shampoo and conditioner are often needed because the breed has a tendency towards dry skin and coat. Pubescent dogs, usually males, also have a tendency to develop chin acne, and medicated shampoos, scrubs and gels are usually necessary.

BEHAVIOR AND PERSONALITY OF THE ACTIVE BOXER

Behavior and personality are two qualities which are hard to standardize within a breed. Although generalizations are difficult to make, most Boxers are alert, loyal and people-oriented. They make great working dogs because they do have the capacity to be loyal, determined, watchful and obedient. However, it is their social nature that makes them want to work with people. This is not the breed to be tied in the backyard to serve as a watchdog. Whether they are shy or vicious has something to do with their genetics, but also is determined by the socialization and training they receive. Most Boxers are extremely playful yet gentle with children but will be fiercely protective around strangers. An old German saying states that "the Boxer fears neither death nor the devil."

Behavior and personality are incredibly important in dogs, and there seem to be quite evident extremes in the Boxer. The earliest of the breed were bred for aggression and that didn't make them ideal house pets. They were working dogs. Today's Boxers seem far removed from their earliest ancestors. The ideal personality problems. It is also imperative that *all* Boxers be obedience trained. Like any dog, they have the potential to be vicious without appropriate training; consider obedience classes mandatory for your sake

Many Boxers enjoy an afternoon nap, and it's even better with a friend. Sammy shares a snooze with six-month-old Kelly Ann.

Boxer is neither aggressive nor neurotic but rather a loving family member with good self-esteem and acceptance of position in the family "pack." Because the Boxer is a powerful dog and can cause much damage, it is worth spending the time when selecting a pup to pay attention to any evidence of

and that of your dog.

Although many Boxers are happy to sleep the day away in bed or on a sofa, most enjoy having a purpose in their day, and that makes them excellent working dogs. They like long daily walks and they do appreciate events that involve family members. Do not let Boxer pups

Well rested from his nap, Sammy is ready for some outdoor playtime! Scott, his owner, is one of his favorite playmates.

run unrestricted because it can increase their risk of developing orthopedic disorders. All Boxers should attend obedience classes and they need to learn limits to unacceptable behaviors. A well-loved and well-controlled Boxer is certain to be a valued family member.

For pet owners, there are several activities to which your Boxer is well-suited. They not only make great walking and jogging partners, but they are also excellent community volunteers; they can visit hospitals, homes for the aged and schools.

The breed seems ideally suited to standing still for kisses, hugs and petting that can last for hours at a time. The loyal and loving Boxer will instinctively be your personal guard dog if properly trained; aggressiveness and viciousness do not fit into the equation.

For Boxer enthusiasts who want to get into more competitive aspects of the dog world, conformation showing, obedience, guarding, and tracking, are all activities that can be considered.

Boxers are well suited to a wide variety of activities. Starview's Kafka, CDX, takes a hike with owner Josie O'Reilly.

SELECTING

**WHAT YOU NEED TO KNOW TO FIND
THE BEST BOXER PUPPY**

Owning the perfect Boxer rarely happens by accident. On the other hand, owning a genetic dud is almost always the result of an impulse

purchase and failure to do even basic research. Buying this book is a major step in understanding the situation and making intelligent choices.

Facing page: Selecting a puppy is a hard enough decision—having a litter of Boxer puppies to choose from doesn't make it any easier, especially when they're all perfect like these Jacquet pups bred by Rick Tomita.

SOURCES

Recently, a large survey was done to determine whether there were more problems seen in animals adopted from pet stores, breeders, private owners or animal shelters. Somewhat surprisingly, there didn't appear to be any major difference in total number of problems seen from these sources. What was different were the kinds of problems seen in each source. Thus, you can't rely on any one source because there are no standards by which judgments can be

The adorable face of a Boxer puppy can be quite persuasive—however, puppy ownership is a big responsibility and requires an informed choice based on more than just "cuteness."

made. Most veterinarians will recommend that you select a "good breeder" but there is no way to identify such an individual. A breeder of champion show dogs may also be a breeder of genetic defects.

The best approach is to select a pup from a source that regularly performs genetic screening and has documentation to prove it. If you are intending to be a pet owner, don't worry about whether your pup is show quality. A mark here or there that might disqualify the pup as a show winner has absolutely no impact on its ability to be a loving and healthy pet. Also, the vast majority of dogs will be neutered and not used for breeding anyway. Concentrate on the things that are important.

MEDICAL SCREENING

Whether you are dealing with a breeder, a breed rescue group, a shelter or a pet store, your approach should be the same. You want to identify a Boxer that you can live with and screen it for medical and behavioral problems before you make it a permanent family member. If the source you select has not done the important testing needed, make sure the individual or organization will offer you a health/temperament guarantee before you remove the dog from the premises to have the work done yourself. If this is not acceptable, or they are offering an exchange-only policy, keep moving; this isn't the right place for you to get a dog. As soon as you purchase a Boxer, pup or adult, go to your veterinarian for thorough evaluation and testing.

inbreeding at least three generations back in the puppy's pedigree. Also ask the breeder to provide OFA, GDC and CERF registration numbers on all ancestors in the pedigree for which testing is done. If there are a lot of gaps, the breeder has some explaining to do.

The screening procedure is easier if you select an older dog.

A puppy should always be purchased from a reputable source—one that can provide the buyer with information on the pup's medical and genetic background.

Pedigree analysis is best left to true enthusiasts but there are some things that you can do, even as a novice. Inbreeding is to be discouraged, so check out your four- or five-generation pedigree and look for names that appear repeatedly. Reputable breeders will usually not allow

Animals can be registered for hips and elbows as young as two years of age by the Orthopedic Foundation for Animals and by one year of age by the Institute for Genetic Disease Control in Animals. This is your insurance against hip dysplasia and elbow dysplasia later in life. Although

Boxers now have a relatively low incidence of these orthopedic problems, it is because of the efforts of conscientious breeders who have been doing the appropriate testing. A verbal testimonial that they've never heard of the condition in their lines is not adequate and probably means they really don't know if they have a problem. Move along.

Evaluation is somewhat more complicated in the Boxer puppy. The PennHip™ procedure can determine risk for developing hip dysplasia in pups as young as 16 weeks of age. For pups younger than that, you should request copies of OFA or GDC registration for both parents. If the parents haven't both been registered, their hip and elbow status should be considered unknown and questionable.

All Boxers, regardless of age, should be screened for evidence of von Willebrand's disease. This can be accomplished with a simple blood test. The incidence is high enough in the breed that there is no excuse for not performing the test.

For animals older than one year of age, your veterinarian will also want to take a blood sample to check for thyroid function in addition to von Willebrand's disease. A heartworm test, urinalysis and evaluation of feces for internal parasites is also indicated. If there are any patches of hair loss, a skin scraping should be taken to determine if the dog has evidence of demodectic mange.

Your veterinarian should also perform a very thorough ophthalmologic (eye) examination. The most common eye problems in Boxers are cataracts, refractory superficial corneal ulcers and retinal dysplasia. It is best to acquire a pup whose parents have both been screened for heritable eye diseases and certified "clear" by organizations such as CERF (Canine Eye Registration Foundation). If this has been the case, an examination by your veterinarian is probably sufficient and referral to an ophthalmologist is only necessary if recommended by your veterinarian.

BEHAVIORAL SCREENING

Medical screening is important, but don't forget about temperament. More dogs are killed each year for behavioral reasons than for all medical problems combined. Temperament testing is a valuable although not infallible tool in the screening process. The reason that temperament is so important is that many dogs are eventually destroyed because they exhibit undesirable behaviors. Although not all behaviors are evident in young pups (e.g., aggression often takes many months to manifest itself), detecting anxious and fearful pups (and avoiding them) can be very important in the selection process. Traits most identifiable in the young pup include: fear; excitability; low pain threshold; extreme submission; and noise sensitivity. There are many different techniques available and a complete discussion is beyond the scope of this book.

Pups can be evaluated for temperament as early as 7–8 weeks of age. Some behaviorists, breeders and trainers recommend objective testing where scores are given in several different categories. Others are more casual about the process since it only a crude indicator anyway. In general, the evaluation takes place in three stages by someone the pup has not been exposed to. The testing is not done within 72 hours of vaccination or surgery. First, the pup is observed and handled to determine its sociability. Puppies with obvious undesirable traits such as shyness, hyperactivity or uncontrollable biting may turn out to be unsuitable. Second, the desired pup is separated from the others and

Temperament is hereditary to some extent, but it also depends heavily on how the pups are raised and socialized. This five-week-old Boxer wants her littermate to wake up and play!

then observed for how it responds when played with and called. Third, the pup should be stimulated in various ways and its responses noted. Suitable activities include lying the pup on its side, grooming it, clipping its nails, gently grasping it around the muzzle and testing its reactions to noise. In a study conducted at the Psychology Department of Colorado State University, the staff also found that heart rate was a good indicator in this third stage of evaluation. Actually, they noted the resting heart rates, stimulated the pups with a loud noise and measured how long it took the heart rates to recover to resting levels. Most pups recovered within 36 seconds. Dogs that took considerably longer were more likely to be anxious.

Puppy Aptitude Tests (PAT) can be given, in which a numerical score is given for eleven different traits, with a "1" representing the most assertive or aggressive expression of a trait and a "6" representing disinterest, independence or inaction. The traits assessed in the PAT include: social attraction to people; following; restraint; social dominance; elevation (lifting off ground by evaluator); retrieve; touch sensitivity; sound sensitivity; prey/chase drive; sta-

bility; and energy level. Although the tests do not absolutely predict behaviors, they do tend to do well at predicting puppies at behavioral extremes.

ORGANIZATIONS YOU SHOULD KNOW ABOUT

Project TEACH™ (Training and Education in Animal Care and Health) is a voluntary accreditation process for those individuals selling animals to the public. It is administered by Pet Health Initiative, Inc. (PHI) and provides instruction on genetic screening as well as many other aspects of proper pet care. TEACH-accredited sources screen animals for a variety of medical, behavioral and infectious diseases *before* they are sold. Project TEACH™ supports the efforts of registries such as OFA, GDC and CERF and recommends that all animals sold be registered with the appropriate agencies. For more information on Project TEACH™, send a self-addressed stamped envelope to Pet Health Initiative, P.O. Box 12093, Scottsdale, AZ 85267-2093.

The Orthopedic Foundation for Animals (OFA) is a nonprofit organization established in 1966 to collect and disseminate information concerning orthopedic diseases of animals and to es-

"Hey...no pushing!" Anthony and Andrew MacDonald share their slide with seven-month-old Nala. All three are "children" of Wendy MacDonald.

tablish control programs to lower the incidence of orthopedic diseases in animals. A registry is maintained for both hip dysplasia and elbow dysplasia. The ultimate purpose of OFA certification is to provide information to dog owners to assist in the selection of good breeding animals; therefore, attempts to get a dysplastic dog certified will only hurt the breed by perpetuation of the disease. For more information, contact your veterinarian or the

Orthopedic Foundation for Animals, 2300 Nifong Blvd., Columbia, MO 65201.

The Institute for Genetic Disease Control in Animals (GDC) is a nonprofit organization founded in 1990 and maintains an open registry for orthopedic problems but does not compete with OFA. In an open registry like GDC, owners, breeders, veterinarians, and scientists can trace the genetic history of any particular dog once that dog and close relatives have been registered. At the present time, the GDC operates open registries for hip dysplasia, elbow dysplasia, and osteochondrosis. The GDC is currently developing guidelines for registries of: Legg-Calve-Perthes disease, craniomandibular osteopathy, and medial patellar luxation. For more information, contact the Institute for Genetic Disease Control in Animals, P.O. Box 222, Davis, CA 95617.

The Canine Eye Registration Foundation (CERF) is an international organization devoted to eliminating hereditary eye diseases from purebred dogs. This organization is similar to

At seven-and-a-half weeks of age, Kafka looks a little bit overwhelmed by his surroundings. Owned by Josie O'Reilly.

At three months of age, Kafka is growing up into a strong and healthy Boxer who's ready to make his mark on the world!

OFA, which helps eliminate diseases like hip dysplasia. CERF is a non-profit organization that screens and certifies purebreds as free of heritable eye diseases. Dogs are evaluated by veterinary eye specialists and findings are then submitted to CERF for documentation. The goal is to identify purebreds without heritable eye problems so they can be used for breeding. Dogs being considered for breeding programs should be screened and certified by CERF on an annual basis, since not all problems are evident in puppies. For more information on CERF, write to CERF, SCC-A, Purdue University, West Lafayette, IN 47907.

FEEDING & NUTRITION

**WHAT YOU MUST CONSIDER EVERY DAY TO FEED
YOUR BOXER THROUGH HIS LIFETIME**

Nutrition is one of the most important aspects of raising a healthy Boxer and yet it is often the source of much controversy between breeders, veterinarians, pet owners and dog food manufacturers. However, most of these ar-guments have more to do with marketing than with science.

Facing page: Good nutrition is as important for dogs as it is for humans. A Boxer needs to be fed a balanced, nutrient-rich diet in order to maintain good health. Owned by Rick Tomita.

Let's first take a look at dog foods and then determine the needs of a dog. This chapter will concentrate of feeding the pet Boxer rather than breeding or working animals.

COMMERCIAL DOG FOODS

Most dog foods are sold based on marketing (i.e., how to make a product appealing to owners while meeting the needs of dogs). Some foods are marketed on the basis of their protein content; others based on a "special" ingredient, and some are sold because they don't contain certain ingredients (e.g., preservatives, soy). We want a dog food that specifically meets our dog's needs, is economical and causes few, if any, problems. Most foods come in dry, semi-moist and canned forms. Some can now be purchased frozen. The "dry" foods are the most economical, and contain the least fat and the most preservatives. The canned foods are the most expensive (they're 75% water), usually contain the most fat, and have the least preservatives. Semi-moist foods are expensive, high in sugar content and I do not recommend them for any dogs.

When you're selecting a commercial diet, make sure the food has been assessed by feeding trials for a specific life stage, not just by nutrient analysis. This statement is usually located not far from the ingredient label. In the United States, these trials are performed in accordance with American Association of Feed Control Officials (AAFCO) and, in Canada, by the Canadian Veterinary Medical Association. This certification is important because it has been found that dog foods currently on the market that provide only a chemical analysis and calculated values but no feeding trial may not provide adequate nutrition. The feeding trials show that the diets meet minimal, not optimal, standards. However, they are the best tests we currently have.

PUPPY REQUIREMENTS

Soon after pups are born, and certainly within the first 24 hours, they should begin nursing their mother. This provides them with colostrum, which is an antibody-rich milk that helps protect them from infection for their first few months of life. Pups should be allowed to nurse for at least six weeks before they are completely weaned from their mother. Supplemental feeding may be started by as early as three weeks of age.

By two months of age, pups should be fed puppy food. They

are now in an important growth phase. Nutritional deficiencies and/or imbalances during this time of life are more devastating that at any other time. Also, this is not the time to overfeed pups or provide them with "performance" rations. Overfeeding Boxers can lead to serious skeletal defects such as osteochondrosis and hip dysplasia.

Pups should be fed "growth" diets until they are 12–18 months of age. Many Boxers do not mature until 18 months of age and so benefit from a longer period on these rations. Pups will initially need to be fed 2–3 meals daily until they are 12–18 months old, then once to twice daily (preferably twice) when they are converted to adult food.

Nursing puppies receive colostrum, an antibody-rich milk produced by the dam to protect the pups from disease in their first months of life.

Proper growth diets should be selected based on acceptable feeding trials designed for growing pups. If you can't tell by reading the label, ask your veterinarian for feeding advice.

Remember that pups need "balance" in their diets and avoid the temptation to supplement with protein, vitamins, or minerals. Calcium supplements sible for many bone deformities seen in these growing dogs.

ADULT DIETS

The goal of feeding adult dogs is one of "maintenance." They have already done the growing they are going to do and are unlikely to have the digestive problems of elderly dogs. In general, dogs can do well on main-

If left to their own devices, Boxer puppies might just cook something up for themselves. It's up to you, the owner, to make sure they get the nutrition they need.

have been implicated as a cause of bone and cartilage deformity, especially in large-breed puppies. Puppy diets are already heavily fortified with calcium, and supplements tend to unbalance the mineral intake. There is more than adequate proof that these supplements are respon- tenance rations containing predominantly plant or animal-based ingredients as long as that ration has been specifically formulated to meet maintenance level requirements. This contention should be supported by studies performed by the manufacturer in accordance with AAFCO

(American Association of Feed Control Officials). In Canada, these products should be certified by the Canadian Veterinary Medical Association to meet maintenance requirements.

There's nothing wrong with feeding cereal-based diets to dogs on maintenance rations and they are the most economical. Soy is a common ingredient in cereal-based diets but may not be completely digested by all dogs, especially Boxers. This causes no medical problems, although Boxers may tend to be more flatulent on these diets. When comparing maintenance rations, it must be appreciated that these diets must meet the "minimum" requirements for confined dogs, not necessarily optimal levels. Most dogs will benefit when fed diets that contain easily digested ingredients that provide nutrients at least slightly above minimum requirements. Typically, these foods will be intermediate in price between the most expensive super-premium diets and the cheapest generic diets. Select only those diets that have been substantiated by feeding trials to meet maintenance requirements, those that contain wholesome ingredients, and those recommended by your veterinarian. Don't select based on price alone,

on company advertising, or on total protein content.

GERIATRIC DIETS

Boxers are considered elderly when they are about seven years of age and there are certain changes that occur as dogs age that alter their nutritional requirements. As pets age, their metabolism slows and this must be accounted for. If maintenance

Adult Boxers need proper nutrition just like puppies do. However, the goal of feeding an adult dog is one of maintenance rather than growth. Owned by Arlene Freer.

rations are fed in the same amounts while metabolism is slowing, weight gain may result. Obesity is the last thing one wants to contend with in an elderly pet, since it increases the risk of several other health-related problems. As pets age, most of their organs function not as well as in youth. The digestive system, the liver, pancreas and gallbladder are not functioning at peak effect. The intestines have more difficulty extracting all the nutrients from the food consumed. A gradual decline in kidney function is considered a normal part of aging.

A responsible approach to geriatric nutrition is to realize that degenerative changes are a normal part of aging. Our goal is to minimize the potential damage done by taking this into account while the dog is still well. If we wait until an elderly dog is ill before we change the diet, we have a much harder job.

Elderly dogs need to be treated as individuals. While some benefit from the nutrition found in "senior" diets, others might do better on the highly digestible puppy and super-premium diets. These latter diets provide an excellent blend of digestibility and amino acid content but, unfortunately, many are higher in salt and phosphorus than the older pet really needs.

Older dogs are also more prone to developing arthritis and therefore it is important not to overfeed them since obesity puts added stress on the joints. For animals with joint pain, supplementing the diet with fatty acid combinations containing cis-linoleic acid, gamma-linolenic acid and eicosapentaenoic acid can be quite beneficial.

MEDICAL CONDITIONS AND DIET

It is important to keep in mind that dietary choices can affect the development of orthopedic diseases such as hip dysplasia and osteochondrosis. When feeding a pup at risk, avoid high-calorie diets and try to feed several times a day rather than ad libitum. Sudden growth spurts are to be avoided because they result in joint instability. Recent research has also suggested that the electrolyte balance of the diet may also play a role in the development of hip dysplasia. Rations that had more balance between the positively and negatively charged elements in the diet (e.g., sodium, potassium, chloride) were less likely to promote hip dysplasia in susceptible dogs. Also avoid supplements of calcium, phosphorus and vitamin D as they can interfere with normal bone and cartilage development. The fact is that calcium levels in the body are carefully regulated by hormones (such as calcitonin and parathormone) as well as vitamin D. Supplementation disturbs this normal regulation and can cause many problems. It has also been shown that calcium supplementation can interfere with the proper absorption of zinc from the intestines. If you really feel the need to supplement your dog, select products such as eicosapentaenoic/gamma-linolenic fatty acid combinations or small amounts of vitamin C.

You can't prevent heart disease in dogs entirely by dietary changes but there are some things that you can do to help. In addition to selecting properly formulated diets, nutritional supplements can be a useful addition in this case. In the Boxer, research has shown that many cases respond to supplements of L-carnitine, an amino acid. Approximately 40% of dogs with dilated cardiomyopathy have a deficiency of L-carnitine in their heart muscle. L-carnitine supplementation is therefore the treatment of choice for these dogs, especially Boxers. A definitive dosage has not been determined, but many veterinary cardiologists use one to two grams, three times daily. L-carnitine is a very safe supplement and is available without a prescription from most health-supply stores. Dogs that respond to L-carnitine usually do so within the first three months of treatment. Clinical improvement is typically seen in the first four weeks but it takes

longer for the changes to be evident on electrocardiograms or echocardiograms. It may also be advisable to begin supplementation with coenzyme Q_{10} by two years of age. A dosage has not been precisely determined for dogs, but some cardi-

High-calorie diets and free feeding are discouraged for the young pup. A balanced diet and regular "mealtimes" are recommended to prevent orthopedic disorders from developing in the growing puppy.

ologists are using doses of 30–90 mg/day. The soft gelatin capsules are preferred and they can be orally administered or punctured and squirted onto the food. This has been shown to improve heart muscle function and may delay the onset of clinical heart disease in susceptible animals.

Diet can't prevent bloat (gastric dilatation-volvulus) but changing feeding habits can

A Boxer that eats healthy will look healthy! A shiny coat and a high-energy level are two indications that your Boxer is getting the nutrition he needs.

make a difference. Initially, the bloat occurs when the stomach becomes distended with swallowed air. This air is swallowed as a consequence of gulping food or water, stress and exercising too close to mealtime. This is where we can make a difference. Divide meals and feed them three times daily rather than all at once. Soak dry dog food in water before feeding to decrease the tendency to gulp the food. If you want to feed dry food only, add some large clean chew toys to the feed bowl so that the dog has to "pick" to get at the food and can't gulp it. Putting the food bowl on a step-stool so the dog doesn't have to stretch to get the food may also be helpful. Finally, don't allow any exercise for at least one hour before and after feeding.

Fat supplements are probably the most common supplements purchased from pet supply stores. They frequently promise to add luster, gloss, and sheen to the coat, and consequently make dogs look healthy. The only fatty acid that is essential for this purpose is cis-linoleic acid, which is found in flaxseed oil, sunflower seed oil, and safflower oil. Corn oil is a suitable but less effective alternative. Most of the other oils found in retail supplements are high in saturated and monounsaturated fats and are not beneficial for shiny fur or healthy skin. For dogs with allergies, arthritis, high blood pressure (hypertension), high cholesterol, and some heart ailments, other fatty acids may be prescribed by a veterinarian: The important ingredients in these products are gamma-linolenic acid (GLA), eicosapentaenoic acid (EPA), and docosahexaenoic acid (DHA). These products have gentle and natural anti-inflammatory properties. But don't be fooled by imitations. Most retail fatty acid supplements do not contain these functional forms of the essential fatty acids—look for gamma-linolenic acid,

Your pup will love you for feeding him right. Rick Tomita gets a puppy kiss from one of his young Boxers.

eicosapentaenoic acid, and docosahexaenoic acid on the label.

The Carrot Bone™ by Nylabone® is the "natural" choice for a healthy doggie snack. It's a nutritious way to keep your Boxer busy between meals, and it's totally edible.

HEALTH

**PREVENTIVE MEDICINE AND HEALTH
CARE FOR YOUR BOXER**

Keeping your Boxer healthy requires preventive health care. This is not only the most effective, but the least expensive way to battle illness. Good preventive  tive care starts even before puppies are born. The dam should be well cared for, vaccinated and free of infections and parasites.

Facing page: Your Boxer will be a part of your family for many years to come. Good preventive care starts with understanding your Boxer's health needs at each stage of his life.

Hopefully, both parents were screened for important genetic diseases (e.g., von Willebrands's disease), registered with the appropriate agencies (e.g., OFA, GDC, CERF), showed no evidence of medical or behavioral problems and were found to be good candidates for breeding. This gives the pup a good start in life. If all has been planned well, the dam will pass on resistance to disease to her pups that will last for the first few months of life. However, the dam can also pass on parasites, infections, genetic diseases and more.

TWO TO THREE WEEKS OF AGE

By two to three weeks of life, it is usually necessary to start pups on a regimen to control worms. Although dogs benefit from this parasite control, the primary reason for doing this is human health. After whelping, the dam often sheds large numbers of worms even if she tested negative previously. This is because many worms lay dormant in tissues and the stress of delivery causes parasite release and shedding into the environment. Assume that all puppies potentially

One-day-old Boxer puppies nurse from their mother, Rascal's Julia Miela. This is only part of the litter—there were eleven puppies in all!

have worms because studies have shown that 75% do. Thus, we institute worm control early to protect the people in the house from worms more than the pups themselves. The deworming is repeated every two to three weeks until your veterinarian feels the condition is under control. Nursing bitches should be treated at the same time because they often shed worms during this time. Only use products recommended by your veterinarian. Over-the-counter parasiticides have been responsible for deaths in pups.

SIX TO TWENTY WEEKS OF AGE

Most puppies are weaned from their mother at six to eight weeks of age. Weaning shouldn't be done too early so that pups have the opportunity to socialize with their littermates and dam. This is important for them to be able to respond to other dogs later in life. There is no reason to rush the weaning process unless the dam can't produce enough milk to feed the pups.

Pups are usually first examined by their veterinarian at six to eight weeks of age which is when most vaccination schedules commence. If pups are exposed to many other dogs at this

young age, veterinarians often opt for vaccinating with inactivated parvovirus at six weeks of age. When exposure isn't a factor, most veterinarians would rather wait to see the pup at eight weeks of age. At this point, they can also do a preliminary dental evaluation to see that all

A puppy as tiny as this little Boxer can't take care of himself. He needs a caring and responsible owner who will make sure that he gets the best care right from day one.

the puppy teeth are coming in correctly, check to see that the testicles are properly descending in males and that there are no health reasons to prohibit vaccination at this time. Heart murmurs, wandering knee-caps (luxating patellae), juvenile cataracts, persistent hyperplastic primary vitreous (a congenital eye disease) and hernias are usually evident by this time.

Your veterinarian may also be able to perform temperament testing on the pup by eight weeks of age, or recommend someone to do it for you. Although temperament testing is not completely accurate, it can often predict which pups are most anx-

study done at the University of Florida College of Veterinary Medicine over a span of more than four years concluded there was no increase in complications when animals were neutered when less than six months of age. The evaluators also concluded that the surgery appeared to be less stressful when done in young pups.

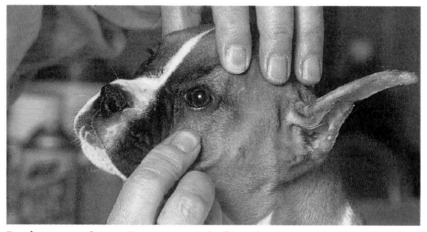

During one of your Boxer puppy's first check ups, the veterinarian will examine his eyes to check for symptoms of juvenile cataracts or any other congenital eye disorders.

ious and fearful. Some form of temperament evaluation is important because behavioral problems account for more animals being euthanized (killed) each year than all medical conditions combined.

Recently, some veterinary hospitals have been recommending neutering pups as early as six to eight weeks of age. A

Most vaccination schedules consist of injections being given at 6-8, 10-12 and 14-16 weeks of age. Ideally, vaccines should not be given closer than two weeks apart and three to four weeks seems to be optimal. Each vaccine usually consists of several different viruses (e.g., parvovirus, distemper, parainfluenza, hepatitis) combined into one injection. Coronavirus can be given as a separate vaccination according to this same schedule if pups are at risk. Some veterinarians and breeders advise another parvovirus booster at 18–20 weeks of age. A booster is given for all vaccines at one year of age and annually thereafter. For animals at increased initial series consists of 3–4 injections spaced 2–3 weeks apart, starting as early as 10 weeks of age. Rabies vaccine is given as a separate injection at three months of age, then repeated when the pup is one year old, then every one to three years depending on local risk and government regulation.

Puppies usually begin receiving vaccinations between six and eight weeks of age. Your veterinarian will recommend an appropriate vaccination schedule for your Boxer puppy.

risk of exposure, parvovirus vaccination may be given as often as four times a year. A new vaccine for canine cough (tracheobronchitis) is squirted into the nostrils. It can be given as early as six weeks of age if pups are at risk. Leptospirosis vaccination is given in some geographic areas and likely offers protection for 6–8 months. The

Between 8 and 14 weeks of age, use every opportunity to expose the pup to as many people and situations as possible. This is part of the critical socialization period that will determine how good a pet your dog will become. This is not the time to abandon a puppy for eight hours while you go to work. This is also not the time to punish your dog in any way, shape or form.

This is the time to introduce your dog to neighborhood cats, birds and other creatures. Hold off on exposure to other dogs until after the second vaccination in the series. You don't want your new friend to pick up contagious diseases from dogs it meets in its travels before it has adequate protection. By 12 weeks of age, your pup should be ready for social outings with other dogs. Do them—they're a great way for your dog to feel comfortable around members of its own species. Walk the streets and introduce your pup to everybody you meet. Your goal should be to introduce your dog to every type of person or situation it is likely to encounter in its life. Take it in cars, elevators, buses, travel crates, subways, parade grounds, beaches; you want it to habituate to all environments. Expose your pup to kids, teenagers, old people, people in wheelchairs, people on bicycles, people in uniforms. The more varied the exposure, the better the socialization.

Proper identification of your pet is also important since this minimizes the risk of theft and increases the chances that your pet will be returned to you if it is lost. There are several different options. Microchip implantation is a relatively painless procedure involving the subcutaneous injection of an implant the size of a grain of rice. This implant does not act as a beacon if your pet goes missing. However, if your pet turns up at a veterinary clinic or shelter and is checked with a scanner, the chip provides information about the owner that can be used to quickly reunite you with your pet. This method of identification is reasonably priced, permanent in nature, and performed at most veterinary clinics. Another option is tattooing, which can be done on the inner ear or on the skin of the

After his second set of vaccinations, your Boxer should be ready to go out and make new friends. This Boxer shares his Gumabone® Frisbee®* with an Australian Shepherd pal.
*The trademark Frisbee is used under license from Mattel, Inc., CA, USA.

abdomen. Most purebreds are given a number by the associated registry (e.g., American Kennel Club, United Kennel Club, Canadian Kennel Club) and this is used for identification. Alternatively, permanent numbers such as social security numbers (telephone numbers and addresses may change during the life of your pet) can be used in the tattooing process. There are several different tattoo registries maintaining lists of dogs, their tattoo codes and their owners. Finally, identifying collars and tags provide quick information but can be separated from your pet if it is lost or stolen. They work best when combined with a permanent identification system such as microchip implantation or tattoo.

FOUR TO SIX MONTHS OF AGE

At 16 weeks of age, when your pup gets the last in its series of regular induction vaccinations, ask your veterinarian about evaluating the pup for hip dysplasia with the PennHip™ technique. This helps predict the risk of developing hip dysplasia as well as degenerative joint disease. Boxer breeders have done an excellent job decreasing the incidence of hip dysplasia through routine screening and

registration programs. Since anesthesia is typically required for the procedure, many veterinarians like to do the evaluation at the same time as neutering.

At this same time, it is very worthwhile to perform a diagnostic test for von Willebrand's disease, an inherited disorder that causes uncontrolled bleeding. A simple blood test is all that is required, but it may need to be sent to a special laboratory

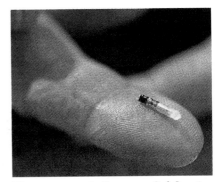

The newest form of ident-ification is microchipping. The microchip is a computer chip that is no bigger than a grain of rice.

to have the test performed. You will be extremely happy you had the foresight to have this done before neutering. If your dog does have a bleeding problem, it will be necessary to take special precautions during surgery.

As a general rule, neuter your animal at about six months of age unless you fully intend to breed it. As mentioned earlier, neutering can be safely done at eight weeks of age but this is still not a common practice. Neutering not only stops the possibility of pregnancy and undesirable behaviors, but can prevent several health problems as well. It is a well established fact that pups spayed before their first heat have a dramatically reduced incidence of mammary (breast) cancer. Neutered males

heartworm prevention therapy. Some veterinarians are even recommending preventive therapy in younger pups. This might be a one-a-day regimen, but newer therapies can be given on a once-a-month basis. As a bonus, most of these heartworm preventatives also help prevent internal parasites.

If your Boxer has any patches of hair loss, your veterinarian will want to perform a skin scraping with a scalpel blade to see if *Demodex* mites are responsible. If there is a problem, don't lose hope; about 90% of demodicosis cases can be cured with supportive care only. However, it's important to diagnose it early before scarring results.

Nylafloss® is a great way to teach puppies healthy chewing habits. It is especially helpful for promoting correct tooth development as it aids in the removal of baby teeth.

significantly decrease their incidence of prostate disorders.

Also when your pet is six months of age, your veterinarian will want to take a blood sample to perform a heartworm test. If the test is negative and shows no evidence of heartworm infection, the pup will go on

Another part of the six-month visit should be a thorough dental evaluation to make sure all the permanent teeth have correctly erupted. If they haven't, this will be the time to correct the problem. Correction should only be performed to make the animal more comfortable and promote more normal chewing. The pro-

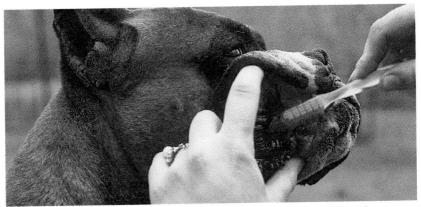

Good dental care for your Boxer begins at home. Brushing your dog's teeth on a regular basis will lessen the need for your veterinarian to perform extensive dental work.

cedures should never be used to cosmetically improve the appearance of a dog used for show purposes or breeding.

After the dental evaluation, you should start implementing home dental care. In most cases, this will consist of brushing the teeth one or more times each week and perhaps using dental rinses. It is a sad fact that 85% of dogs over four years of age have periodontal disease and doggy breath. In fact, it is so common that most people think it is "normal." Well, it is normal—as nor-

Roar-Hide™ by Nylabone® is a rawhide chew product that is melted and molded to be safe for your Boxer. It is 86.2% protein and 100% edible.

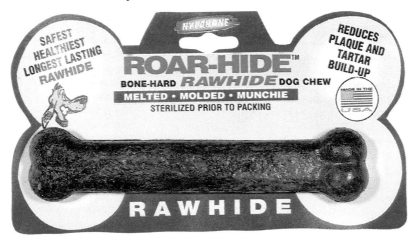

mal as bad breath would be in people if they never brushed their teeth. Brush your dog's teeth regularly with a special tooth brush and toothpaste and you can greatly reduce the incidence of tartar buildup, bad breath and gum disease. Better preventive care means that dogs live a long time. They'll enjoy their sunset years more if they still have their teeth. Ask your veterinarian for details on home dental care.

ONE TO SEVEN YEARS OF AGE

At one year of age, your dog should be re-examined and have boosters for all vaccines. Your veterinarian will also want to do a very thorough physical examination to look for early evidence of problems. This might include taking radiographs (x-rays) of the hips and elbows to look for evidence of dysplastic changes. Genetic Disease Control (GDC) will certify hips and elbows at 12 months of age; Orthopedic Foundation for Animals won't issue certification until 24 months of age.

At 12 months of age, it's also a great time to have some blood samples analyzed to provide background information. Although few Boxers experience clinical problems at this young age, trouble may be starting. Therefore, it is a good idea to have baseline levels of thyroid hormones (free and total), endogenous TSH (thyroid-stimulating hormone), blood cell counts, organ chemistries, parvovirus antibody titers and cholesterol levels. This can serve as a valuable comparison to samples collected in the future.

Each year, preferably around the time of your pet's birthday, it's time for another veterinary visit. This visit is a wonderful opportunity for a thorough clinical examination rather than just "shots." Since 85% of dogs have periodontal disease by four years of age, veterinary intervention does not seem to be as widespread as it should be. The examination should include visually inspecting the ears; eyes (a great time to start scrutinizing for progressive retinal atrophy, cataracts, etc.); mouth (don't wait for gum disease); and groin; listening (auscultation) to the lungs and heart; feeling (palpating) the lymph nodes and abdomen and answering all of your questions about optimal health care. In addition, booster vaccinations are given during these times, feces are checked for parasites, urine is analyzed and blood samples may be collected for analysis. One of the tests run on the blood sample is for heartworm antigen. In areas of the country where heartworm is only present in the spring, summer and fall (it's spread by mosquitoes), blood samples are collected and evaluated about a month prior to the mosquito season. Other routine blood tests are for blood cells (hematology), organ chemistries, thyroid levels and electrolytes.

By two years of age, most veterinarians prefer to begin preventive dental cleanings, often referred to as "prophies." Anesthesia is required and the veterinarian or veterinary dentist will use an ultrasonic scaler to remove plaque and tartar from above and below the gum line and polish the teeth so that plaque has a harder time sticking to the teeth. Radiographs (x-rays) and fluoride treatments are other options. It is now known that it is plaque, not tartar, that initiates inflammation in the gums. Since scaling and root planing remove more tartar than plaque, veterinary dentists have begun using a new technique called PerioBUD (Periodontal Bactericidal Ultrasonic Debridement). The ultrasonic treatment is quicker, disrupts more bacteria and is less irritating to the gums. With tooth polishing to finish up the procedure, gum healing is better and owners can start home care sooner. Each dog has its own dental needs that must be addressed, but most veterinary dentists recommend prophies annually.

At four to five years of age, your veterinarian will probably want to start screening for dilated cardiomyopathy, since this is very common in Boxers. Chest radiographs (x-rays) aren't usually too helpful; ultrasound examinations (echocardiography) and electrocardiograms (EKGs) are the preferred tests. Annual tests are usually sufficient and it is extremely important to diagnose the condition early because it is such a devastating and life-threatening disease.

SENIOR BOXERS

Boxers are considered seniors when they reach about seven years of age. Veterinarians still usually only need to examine them once a year, but it is now important to start screening for geriatric problems. Accordingly, blood profiles, urinalysis, chest radiographs (x-rays) and electrocardiograms (EKG) are recommended on an annual basis. When problems are caught early, they are much more likely to be successfully managed. This is as true in canine medicine as it is in human medicine.

MEDICAL PROBLEMS

RECOGNIZED GENETIC CONDITIONS SPECIFICALLY RELATED TO THE BOXER

M any conditions appear to be especially prominent in Boxers. Sometimes it is possible to identify the genetic basis of a problem, but in many cases, we must be satisfied with merely identifying the breeds that are a risk and how the conditions can be identified, treated and prevented.

Facing pages: All breeds are prone to specific medical problems, and the Boxer is no exception. Understanding the conditions that affect the Boxer is the key to early detection of a problem.

Following are some conditions that have been recognized as being common in the Boxer but this listing is certainly not complete. Also, many genetic conditions may be common in certain breed lines, not in the breed in general.

ACNE

Acne is not simply a bacterial infection. Certain breeds, such as the Boxer, are particularly at risk. Like the situation in people, waxy deposits clog up the hair follicles (pores), especially in the chin area. Most affected dogs, not surprisingly, start to have problems during puberty and there is usually some reprieve by about three years of age.

Acne does not respond well to antibiotics, and these are not needed for successful treatment. Gentle cleansing pads that are sold for use in people can help clear debris from the clogged pores. Warm poultices can help bring the pus accumulation to a head. In some recalcitrant cases, topical benzoyl peroxide scrubs and gels are helpful; vitamin A-derived retinoid creams can also be helpful. Treatment should not be overdone because this is a cosmetic disorder and doesn't affect the health of the animal.

AORTIC STENOSIS

Aortic stenosis is a hereditary heart disease characterized by an obstruction below the aortic valve. At least two genes are involved in the process, one of which is dominant. Because of the pattern of inheritance, there tends to be a family history of the problem. Many pups may appear fine at first, while others may exhibit weakness, fainting or even sudden death. The diagnosis can be made relatively easily by thorough veterinary exami-

Chin acne in a Boxer. The Boxer is one of the breeds most susceptible to this condition, and although treatment is necessary, it should be remembered that acne is only a cosmetic disorder and not debilitating to the dog.

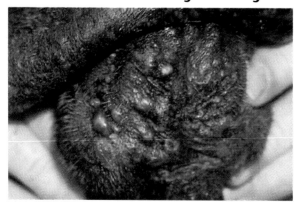

nation with stethoscope (auscultation), x-rays (radiography), electrocardiography (ECG) and/or ultrasound examination (echocardiography). Some mildly affected animals may be fine without therapy, while others require medications (e.g., beta blockers) or corrective surgery by six months of age. Thorough examination of the parents will determine (in most cases) the responsible individual. Even normal littermates should not be used in breeding programs.

BLEEDING DISORDERS

Boxers are prone to several different bleeding disorders, including von Willebrand's disease (covered separately), Factor VII deficiency, and Prothrombin disorder. Factor VII deficiency is an autosomal, incompletely dominant trait, while Prothrombin disorder relates to an autosomal defect of vitamin K-dependent Prothrombin regulation. Both of these can result in bruising and prolonged bleeding. The diagnosis can be confirmed by performing clotting profiles. The best routine screening procedure involves an activated partial thromboplastin time (or Activated Clotting Time) and Prothrombin time (PT). The Prothrombin time will be abnormal

for both conditions, while the Partial Thromboplastin Time (and Activated Clotting Time) will be prolonged for Prothrombin disorder but normal for Factor VII deficiency. Specific tests can be performed for these factors if your veterinarian feels it is warranted. Treatment is sup-

Boxers affected by certain medical conditions can still lead normal, active lives with proper treatment and care.

portive when animals have bleeding episodes and there are no cures. For affected animals it is best to reduce risk by avoiding elective surgery, rough play, internal/external parasites and medications that may affect clotting (such as aspirin).

CANCER

Boxers have the dubious distinction of being the breed most prone to developing cancers. The reasons are uncertain but the conclusion is a definite fact. Not all of the tumors to which they are susceptible are malignant (e.g., histiocytomas are benign and spontaneously resolve), but many are (such as mast-cell tumor). Each form of cancer has its own tendencies, so it is impossible to make generalizations. However, since the overall incidence of cancer is so prevalent in the breed, it makes sense to select breeding stock from lines that have not been affected with cancer.

DEMODICOSIS

Demodex mites are present on the skin of all dogs but in some animals born with a defective immune system the numbers increase and begin to cause problems. Boxers are usually cited as one of the most common breeds affected with this condition. Although it is thought to be genetically transmitted, the mode of transmission has never been conclusively demonstrated.

Most cases of demodicosis are seen in young pups and fully 90% of cases self-cure with little or no medical intervention by the time these dogs reach immu-

nologic maturity at 18–36 months of age. In these cases, it is suspected that the immune system is marginally compromised and eventually matures and gets the condition under control. On the other hand, some pups (about 10% of those initially affected) do not get better and, in fact, become progressively worse. These are thought to have more severe immunologic compromise and are often labeled as having "generalized demodicosis."

The diagnosis is easily made by scraping the skin with a scalpel blade and looking at the collected debris under a microscope. The *Demodex* mites are cigar-shaped and are easily seen. What is harder to identify is the immunologic defect that allowed the condition to occur in the first place. Recent research has suggested the problem may be linked to a decrease in interleukin-2 response, but the genetics is still a question.

If the cause of the immune dysfunction can be cured, the mange will resolve on its own. Likewise, if the pup outgrows its immunologic immaturity or defect, the condition will self-cure. This process can best be assisted by ensuring a healthy diet is being fed, treating for any internal parasites or other diseases, and perhaps using cleansing shampoos and nutritional supplements that help bolster the immune system. However, if the condition does not resolve on its own, or if it is getting worse despite conservative therapy, special mite-killing treatments are necessary. Amitraz is the most common dip used, but experimentally, milbemycin oxime and ivermectin given daily have shown some promising results. It must be remembered that killing the mites will not restore the immune system to normal.

Regarding prevention, it is best not to breed dogs with a history of demodicosis, and dogs with generalized demodicosis should *never* be bred. Although the genetic nature of this disease has not been decisively proven, it doesn't make sense to add affected individuals to the gene pool of future generations.

DILATED CARDIOMYOPATHY

Dilated cardiomyopathy refers to a defect of the heart muscle in which the heart muscle becomes thin and stretched, much like a balloon. In that condition, it is not a very effective pump and, eventually, affected dogs die from heart failure. Boxers are one of the most commonly affected breeds. Thus, this is an extremely important and deadly problem in the breed.

Although a genetic tendency is suspected, long-term studies are not yet available. In Boxers, there appears to be an autosomal genetic association, likely dominant in nature. Studies have also shown that dilated

Boxer pups should be screened for genetic disorders as early as possible since many conditions show few, if any, noticeable symptoms.

cardiomyopathy in this breed is frequently associated with a relative deficiency of the amino acid L-carnitine in heart muscle.

Early in the course of the disease, affected animals seem normal. It is only when they show signs of heart failure that most owners seek veterinary attention. Early signs might include depression, coughing, exercise intolerance, weakness, respiratory distress, decreased appetite, and even fainting. In some breeds and especially in the Boxer, sudden death may be the first clue that something was ever wrong if the animal hasn't had routine veterinary evaluations. Thus, routine thorough veterinary examinations are very important, especially in the young and middle-aged adult.

In some cases the heart rate is increased and this might indicate atrial fibrillation, a common sequel to cardiomyopathy. However, in most cases, radiographs (x-rays), electrocardiograms (EKGs) and echocardiograms (ultrasound examinations) are required for definitive diagnosis. Although dilated cardiomyopathy is frequently associated with L-carnitine deficiency, measuring blood levels of L-carnitine is not helpful. The original connection was made by evaluating L-carnitine con-

centrations in heart muscle, not blood. Radiographs (x-rays) may reveal an enlarged heart. Echocardiograms are painless studies using ultrasound examination, which are extremely useful in making the diagnosis. Electrocardiograms (EKGs) also have their place. Recent studies have shown that most dogs (especially Boxers) with early cardiomyopathy have premature ventricular contractions (PVCs), which are an indicator of increased risk to developing actual cardiomyopathy. These PVCs may not be evident all the time when EKGs are taken, so 24-hour studies with a Holter monitor are sometimes necessary, as they are in people. Studies done to date suggested that the arrhythmias tend to peak in the morning and vary in the afternoon, similar to the situation in people.

There is no cure for cardiomyopathy, but some breeds respond well to mega-doses of specific nutrients. A link to myocardial (heart muscle) L-carnitine deficiency has now been well-studied in the Boxer. Blood levels of L-carnitine are not helpful and the diagnosis was originally reached by heart muscle biopsy. Obviously, this is not a practical diagnostic test. Until there is a better test, all Boxers with dilated cardiomyopathy should be treated with L-carnitine, which is available over-the-counter from health food stores. A precise dosage has not been determined but most cardiologists are recommending one to two grams three times daily. L-carnitine is an extremely safe nutritional supplement but moderately expensive. It may also be worthwhile to supplement with taurine and coenzyme Q_{10} because they have also been demonstrated to be beneficial in cases of cardiomyopathy. For those requiring medical therapy, digoxin (a digitalis derivative) is often used to treat the condition, as are beta-1 blockers and vasodilators. Milrinone, an experimental drug, has been very effective in dogs with heart muscle failure, but is not yet available for dogs or people. All dogs with cardiomyopathy that are treated with drugs only eventually succumb to their disease.

Right now there are no foolproof ways to prevent cardiomyopathy. The best choice is to avoid pups that have a family history of cardiomyopathy. In many cases it will be necessary to know medical history back at least three generations. Preliminary evidence suggests Boxers have an autosomal mode of inheritance that is most likely dominant. A research project funded by the Doberman Pinscher Club of America is trying to determine the genetic link for cardiomyopathy using DNA testing. If that is successful and if the situation is the same in Boxers, it may be possible to prevent the condition by selecting unaffected breeding partners based on tissue testing.

ELBOW DYSPLASIA

Elbow dysplasia doesn't refer to just one disease, but rather an entire complex of disorders that affect the elbow joint. The usual manifestation is a sudden onset of lameness. In time, the continued inflammation results in arthritis in those affected joints.

Fragmented coronoid process of the elbow, a manifestation of elbow dysplasia. Courtesy of Dr. Jack Henry.

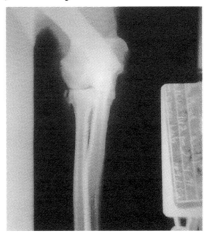

Radiographs (x-rays) are taken of the elbow joints and submitted to a registry for evaluation. The Orthopedic Foundation for Animals (OFA) will assign a breed registry number to those animals with normal elbows that are over 24 months of age. Abnormal elbows are reported as Grade I to III, where Grade III elbows have well-developed degenerative joint disease (arthritis). Normal elbows on individuals 24 months or older are assigned a breed registry number and are periodically reported to parent breed clubs. Genetic Disease Control in Animals (GDC) maintains an open registry for elbow dysplasia and assigns a registry number to those individuals with normal elbows at 12 months of age or older. Only animals with "normal" elbows should be used for breeding.

There is strong evidence to support the contention that OCD of the elbow is an inherited disease, likely controlled by many genes. Preliminary research (in Labrador Retrievers) also suggests that the different forms of elbow dysplasia are inherited independently. Therefore, breeding stock should be selected from those animals without a history of osteochondrosis, preferably for several generations.

Unaffected dogs producing offspring with OCD, FCP or both should not be bred again and unaffected first-degree relatives (e.g., siblings) should not be used for breeding either.

The most likely associations made to date suggest that, other than genetics, feeding diets high in calories, calcium and protein promote the development of osteochondrosis in susceptible dogs. Also, animals that are allowed to exercise in an unregulated fashion are at increased risk, since they are more likely to sustain cartilage injuries.

GASTRIC DILATATION/VOLVULUS (BLOAT)

Gastric dilatation (bloat) occurs when the stomach becomes distended with air. The air gets swallowed into the stomach when susceptible dogs exercise, gulp their food/water or are stressed. Although bloat can occur at any age, it becomes more common as susceptible dogs get older. Purebreds are three times more likely to suffer from bloat than mutts. Boxers are particularly prone to bloat.

Bloat on its own is uncomfortable, but it's the possible consequences that make it life-threatening. As the stomach fills with air like a balloon, it can twist on itself and impede the flow of food within the stomach as well as the blood supply to the stomach and other digestive organs. This twisting (volvulus or torsion) not only makes the bloat worse, but also results in toxins being released into the bloodstream and death of blood-deprived tissues. These events, if allowed to progress, will usually result in death in four to six hours. Approximately one-third of dogs with bloat and volvulus will die, even under appropriate hospital care.

Deep-chested breeds like the Boxer are especially prone to bloat. Precautions can and should be taken to prevent this potentially life-threatening condition from occurring.

Affected dogs will be uncomfortable, restless, depressed and have an extended abdomen. They need veterinary attention immediately or they will suffer from shock and die! There are a variety of surgical procedures to correct the abnormal positioning of the stomach and organs. Intensive medical therapy is also necessary to treat for shock, acidosis and the effects of toxins.

Bloat can't be completely prevented, but there are some easy things to do to greatly reduce risk. Don't leave food down for dogs to eat as they wish. Divide the day's meals into three portions and feed morning, afternoon and evening. Try not to let your dog gulp its food; if necessary, add some chew toys to the bowl so he has to work around these to get the food. Add water to dry food before feeding. Have fresh, clean water available all day but not at mealtime. Do not allow exercise for one hour before and after meals. Following this feeding advice may actually save your dog's life. On the other hand, there have been no studies that support the contention that soy in the diet increases the risk of bloat. Soy is relatively poorly digested and can lead to flatulence, but the gas accumulation in bloat comes from swallowed air, not gas produced in the intestines.

HIP DYSPLASIA

Hip dysplasia is a genetically transmitted developmental problem of the hip joint that is common in many breeds. Dogs may be born with a "susceptibility" or "tendency" to develop hip dysplasia, but it is not a foregone conclusion that all susceptible dogs will eventually develop hip dysplasia. All dysplastic dogs are born with normal hips, and the dysplastic changes begin within the first 24 months of life although they are usually evident long before then.

It is now known that there are several factors that help determine whether a susceptible dog will ever develop hip dysplasia

These include body size, conformation, growth patterns, caloric load and electrolyte balance in the dog food.

Based on research tabulated up to January, 1995, the Orthopedic Foundation for Animals concluded that less than 13.7% of the radiographs submitted from Boxers had evidence of hip dysplasia. This is great news because the Boxer breeders have been able to reduce the incidence in the breed by 40–50% just through conscientious breeding.

When purchasing a Boxer pup, it is best to ensure that the parents were both registered with normal hips through one of the international registries such as the Orthopedic Foundation for Animals or Genetic Disease Control. Pups over 16 weeks of age can be tested by veterinarians trained in the PennHip™ procedure, which is a way of predicting risk of developing hip dysplasia and arthritis. In time it should be possible to completely eradicate hip dysplasia from the breed.

If you start with a pup with less risk of hip dysplasia you can further reduce your risk by controlling its environment. Select a food with a moderate amount of protein and avoid the super-high premium and high-calorie diets. Also, feed your pup several times a day for defined periods (e.g., 15 minutes) rather than leaving the food down all day. Avoid all nutritional supplements, especially those that include calcium, phosphorus and/or vitamin D. Use controlled exercise for your pup rather than letting him run loose. Unrestricted exercise in the pup can stress the joints which are still developing.

If you have a dog with hip dysplasia, all is not lost. There is much variability in the clinical presentation. Some dogs with severe dysplasia experience little pain while others that have minor changes may be extremely sore. The main problem is that dysplastic hips promote degenerative joint disease (osteoarthritis or osteoarthrosis) which can eventually incapacitate the joint. Aspirin and other anti-inflammatory agents are suitable in the early stages; surgery is needed when animals are in great pain, when drug therapy doesn't work adequately, or when movement is severely compromised.

HISTIOCYTIC ULCERATIVE COLITIS

Histiocytic ulcerative colitis is a chronic inflammatory disease

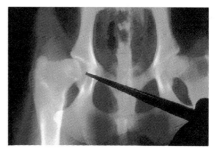

Radiograph of a dog with hip dysplasia. Note the flattened femoral head at the marker. Courtesy of Toronto Academy of Veterinary Medicine, Toronto, Canada.

of the bowel that occurs almost exclusively in the Boxer. The exact cause is not known but a genetic connection is suspected because it runs in lines of dogs, and the incidence has been reduced by selective breeding. A microbial component is also suspected and there are some similarities between this condition and Whipple's disease in people.

Affected Boxers are usually young, often less than two years of age, when they start developing diarrhea and other signs of colitis. The condition is progressive and unrelenting. The diagnosis is confirmed by biopsies of the colon, which reveal ulcers and infiltrations of specific inflammatory cells (histiocytes). There is no cure and the condition should be considered lifelong.

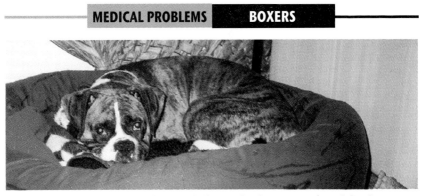

Some Boxers prefer a laid-back lifestyle, but a noticeable decrease in energy or activity level is cause for concern and should be checked out by your veterinarian immediately.

Treatment is supportive using antibiotics such as sulfasalazine, corticosteroids and dietary changes. Most colitis patients are placed on a hypoallergenic diet such as chicken, lamb, egg or cottage cheese with rice or a diet high in fiber. The response is variable and must be tailored for each animal. Because a genetic trend is suspected, affected animals should not be used for breeding.

HYPERADRENOCORTICISM (CUSHING'S SYNDROME)

Hyperadrenocorticism, also known as Cushing's syndrome, results when the body produces too much cortisol, its own form of cortisone. In 85% of cases, the condition results from a tumor (not usually malignant) in the pituitary gland of the brain. The remaining 15% arise from tumors (half are malignant) on the adrenal glands, located near the kidneys. The condition is typically seen in middle-aged to old animals, not pups.

There are a lot of different clinical manifestations to Cushing's syndrome, but the most common are an increase in thirst, hunger and need for urination. Other clinical signs (symptoms) include hair loss, susceptibility to infection, muscle atrophy and lack of energy. There are several different screening tests for Cushing's syndrome but final confirmation usually relies on a dexamethasone suppression test or ACTH stimulation test. Treatment for the pituitary disease is most often attempted with mitotane, ketoconazole or L-deprenyl. For adrenal disease, surgery is most commonly utilized or large doses of the medicines mentioned. Cushing's syndrome in more common in the Boxer, but a specific genetic connection has not been determined. Thus, the best means of prevention is to select dogs from families with no history of the disease.

HYPOTHYROIDISM

Hypothyroidism is the most commonly diagnosed endocrine (hormonal) problem in the Boxer. The disease itself refers to an insufficient amount of thyroid hormones being produced. Although there are several different potential causes, lymphocytic thyroiditis is by far the most common. Iodine deficiency and goiter are extremely rare.

Obesity is *not* a necessary manifestation of hypothyroidism. Many dogs continue to maintain a normal weight while using up their thyroid-hormone reserves.

In lymphocytic thyroiditis, the body produces antibodies that target aspects of thyroid tissue; the process usually starts between one and three years of age in affected animals but doesn't become clinically evident until later in life.

There is a great deal of misinformation about hypothyroidism. Owners often expect their dog to be obese with the condition and otherwise don't suspect it. The fact is that hypothyroidism is quite variable in its manifestations and obesity is only seen in a small percentage of cases. In most cases, affected animals appear fine until they use up most of their remaining thyroid hormone reserves. The most common manifestations then are lack of energy and recurrent infections. Hair loss is seen in about one-third of cases.

You might suspect that hypothyroidism would be easy to diagnose but it is trickier than you think. Since there is a large reserve of thyroid hormones in the body, a test measuring only total blood levels of the hormones (T-4 and T-3) is not a very sensitive indicator of the condition. Thyroid stimulation tests are the best way to measure the functional reserve. Measuring "free" and "total" levels of the hormones and/or endogenous TSH (thyroid-stimulating hormone) are other approaches. Also, since we know that most cases are due to antibodies produced in the body, screening for these autoantibodies can help identify animals at risk of developing hypothyroidism.

Because this breed is so prone to developing hypothyroidism, periodic "screening" for the disorder is warranted in many cases. Although none of the screening tests is perfect, a basic panel evaluating total T-4, free T-4, TSH (thyroid-stimulating hormone) and cholesterol levels is a good start. Ideally, this would first be performed at one year of age and annually thereafter. This "screening" is practical, because none of these tests is very expensive.

Fortunately, although there may be some problems in diagnosing hypothyroidism, treatment is straightforward and relatively inexpensive. Supplementing the affected animal twice daily with thyroid hormone effectively treats the condition. In many breeds, supplementation with thyroid hormones is commonly done to help confirm the diagnosis. However, since thyroid hormones affect the heart, and since Boxers are so prone to the heart disease cardiomyopathy, thyroid hormone supplementation should be reserved for those animals with well-documented hypothyroidism. Animals with hypothyroidism should not be used in a breeding program and those with circulating autoantibodies but no actual hypothyroid disease should also not be used for breeding.

PROGRESSIVE AXONOPATHY

Also known as Boxer Neuropathy, progressive axonopathy is a nerve disease unique to Boxers which is presumed to be transmitted as an autosomal recessive trait. That means that both parents must be carriers for pups to be affected.

Affected pups usually start to have problems by six months of age. First they have awkwardness involving their hindlegs and walk with a stilted gait. Eventually the condition progresses to involve the front legs. To confirm a diagnosis, evoked muscle action potentials are needed and they are typically subnormal; nerve biopsies are another option. There is no cure and affected individuals, their siblings and parents should not be used for breeding.

REFRACTORY SUPERFICIAL CORNEAL ULCERS

Ulcers on the surface of the eye have been commonly reported in Boxers but there are still some unanswered questions regarding cause. Some veterinary ophthalmologists choose to consider the problem as an epithelial basement membrane dystrophy, while others believe it to be a unique Boxer disorder and prefer the generic term "refractory superficial corneal ulcer." Whatever the cause, when the cornea is injured, it takes time to heal. Because of its relatively poor blood supply, the cornea tends to heal more slowly than other tissues.

Most affected Boxers are over five years of age and the majority appear to be spayed bitches. One or both eyes may be affected and that usually means being watery and painful. The ulcer can be highlighted with fluoroscein or Rose Bengal stains making the diagnosis obvious. There is no single treatment that is effective in all cases. Most cases respond initially only to relapse later. Surgery is sometimes required to trim away the damaged cornea and then antibiotics and analgesics are applied as necessary. The eye is re-examined weekly and more of the damaged tissue is trimmed away each time (using a topical anesthetic). Therapeutic contact lenses and collagen corneal bandages have also been used to encourage healing and reduce discomfort. Because the condition is expected to have a genetic basis, affected individuals should not be used for breeding, even if they recover completely.

VON WILLEBRAND'S DISEASE

Von Willebrand's disease (vWD) is the most common inherited bleeding disorder of dogs. The abnormal gene can be inherited from one or both parents. If both parents pass on the gene, most of the resultant pups fail to thrive and most will die. In most cases, though, the pup inherits a relative lack of clotting ability, which is quite variable. For instance, one dog may have 15% of the clotting factor, while another might have 60%. The higher the amount, the less likely it will be that the bleeding will be readily evident since spontaneous bleeding is usually only seen when dogs have less than 30% of the normal level of von Willebrand clotting factor. Thus, some dogs don't get diagnosed until they are neutered or spayed and they end up bleeding uncontrollably or they develop pockets of blood (hematomas) at the surgical site. In addition to the inherited form of vWD, this disorder can also be acquired in association with familial hypothyroidism. This form is usually seen in Boxers older than five years of age.

Inherited disorders are passed on to pups by their parents. The best way to stop the perpetuation of breed-specific diseases is to breed only healthy dogs that are certified as being free of genetic problems.

Von Willebrand's disease is extremely important in the Boxer because the incidence appears to be on the rise. However, there is good news. There are tests available to determine the amount of von Willebrand factor in the blood and they are accurate and reasonably priced. Boxers used for breeding should have normal amounts of von Willebrand factor in their blood and so should all pups that are adopted as household pets. Carriers should not be used for breeding, even if they appear clinically normal. Since hypothyroidism can be linked with von Willebrand's disease, thyroid profiles can also be a useful part of the screening procedure in older Boxers.

A white Boxer is not acceptable for conformation, but this eight-week-old puppy's white coat doesn't affect his potential to become a healthy and loving pet.

OTHER CONDITIONS COMMONLY SEEN IN THE BOXER

- Anesthetic Complications
- Atrial Septal Defect
- Bacterial Endocarditis
- Cataracts
- Central Progressive Retinal Atrophy
- Chemodectoma
- Chondrosarcoma
- Cryptorchidism
- Cutaneous Asthenia
- Cystine Urolithiasis
- Dermoid Sinus
- Distichiasis
- Dystocia
- Ectropion
- Entropion
- Estrogen-Responsive Dermatosis
- Histiocytoma
- Interstitial Cell Tumor
- Gingival Hyperplasia (Epulis)
- Lymphosarcoma
- Mast-Cell Tumor
- Non-Pigmented Third Eyelid
- Osteosarcoma
- Progressive Retinal Atrophy
- Prolapse of Third Eyelid Gland
- Pulmonic Stenosis
- Pyloric Stenosis
- Seasonal Flank Alopecia
- Seminoma
- Sertoli-Cell Tumor
- Vaginal Edema/Prolapse

INFECTIONS & INFESTATIONS

HOW TO PROTECT YOUR BOXER FROM PARASITES AND MICROBES

An important part of keeping your Boxer healthy is to prevent problems caused by parasites and microbes. Although there are a variety of drugs available that can help limit problems, prevention is always the desired option.

Facing page: An itchy Boxer is *not* a happy Boxer! Although there are many products available to treat infestations, it is better to take precautions and avoid a problem in the first place.

FLEAS

Fleas are important and common parasites but not an inevitable part of every pet owner's reality. If you take the time to understand some of the basics of flea population dynamics, control is both conceivable and practical.

Fleas have four life stages (egg, larva, pupa, adult) and each stage responds to some therapies while being resistant to others. Failing to understand this is the major reason why some people have so much trouble getting the upper hand in the battle to control fleas.

Fleas spend all their time on dogs and only leave if physically removed by brushing, bathing or scratching. However, the eggs that are laid on the animal are not sticky and fall to the ground to contaminate the environment. Our goal must be to remove fleas from the animals in the house, from the house itself and from the immediate outdoor environment. Part of our plan must also involve using different medications to get rid of the different life stages as well as minimizing the use of potentially harmful insecticides that could be poisonous for pets and family members.

A flea comb is a very handy device for recovering fleas from pets. The best places to comb are the top of the tail, groin area, armpits, back and neck region. Fleas collected should be dropped into a container of alcohol which quickly kills them before they can escape. In addition, all pets should be bathed with a cleansing shampoo (or flea shampoo) to remove fleas and eggs. This has no residual effect; however, and fleas can jump back on immediately after the bath if nothing else is done. Rather than using potent insecticidal dips and sprays, consider products containing the safe pyrethrins, imidacloprid or fipronil, and the insect growth regulators (such as methoprene and pyripoxyfen) or insect development inhibitors (IDIs) such as lufenuron. These products are not only extremely safe, but the combination is effective against eggs, larvae and adults. This only leaves the pupal stage to cause continued problems. Insect growth regulators can also be safely given as once-a-month oral preparations. Flea collars are rarely useful, and electronic flea collars are not to be recommended for any dogs.

To clean up the household, vacuuming is a good first step because it picks up about 50% of the flea eggs and it also stimulates flea pupae to emerge as

Shampooing is one way to remove fleas from your dog, but it is not guaranteed to kill the itchy critters. The only way to win the battle against fleas is to kill them in all of their life stages.

adults, a stage when they are easier to kill with insecticides. The vacuum bag should then be removed and discarded with each treatment. Household treatment can then be initiated with pyrethrins and a combination of either insect growth regulars or sodium polyborate (a borax derivative). The pyrethrins need to be reapplied every two to three weeks but the insect growth regulators last about two to three months and many companies guarantee so-

dium polyborate for a full year. Stronger insecticides such as carbamates and organophosphates can be used and will last three to four weeks in the household, but they are potentially toxic and offer no real advantages other than their persistence in the home environment. This is also one of their major disadvantages.

When an insecticide is combined with an insect growth regulator, flea control is most likely to be successful. The insecticide kills the adult fleas and the insect growth regulator affects the eggs and larvae. However, insecticides kill less that 20% of flea cocoons (pupae). Because of this, new fleas may hatch in two to three weeks despite appropriate application of products. This is known as the "pupal window" and is one of the most common causes for ineffective flea control. This is why a safe insecticide should be applied to the home environment two to three weeks after the initial treatment. This catches the newly hatched pupae before they have a chance to lay eggs and continue the flea problem.

If treatment of the outdoor environment is needed, there are several options. Pyripoxyfen,

an insect growth regulator, is stable in sunlight and can be used outdoors. Sodium polyborate can be used as well, but it is important that it not be inadvertently eaten by pets. Organophosphates and carbamates are sometimes recommended for outdoor use and it is not necessary to treat the entire property. Flea control should be directed predominantly at garden margins, porches, dog houses, garages, and in other pet lounging areas. Fleas don't do well with direct exposure to sunlight so generalized lawn treatment is not needed. Finally, microscopic worms (nematodes) are available that can be sprayed onto the lawn with a garden sprayer. The nematodes eat immature

Fleas carried into the home by a dog will quickly infest the indoor environment. There are products available that can safely control the flea population inside the home.

flea forms and then biodegrade without harming anything else.

TICKS

Ticks are found worldwide and can cause a variety of problems including blood loss, tick paralysis, Lyme disease, "tick fever," Rocky Mountain Spotted Fever and babesiosis. All are important diseases which need to be prevented whenever possible. This is only possible by limiting the exposure of our pets to ticks.

For those species of tick that dwell indoors, the eggs are laid mostly in cracks and on vertical surfaces in kennels and homes. Otherwise, most other species are found outside in vegetation,

Ears are a favorite place for ticks to hide. Make checking for ticks an important part of your Boxer's regular ear-cleaning routine.

such as grassy meadows, woods, brush, and weeds.

Ticks feed only on blood but they don't actually bite. They attach to an animal by sticking their harpoon-shaped mouth-parts into the

The deer tick is the most common carrier of Lyme disease.

animal's skin and then they suck blood. Some ticks can increase their size 20 to 50 times as they feed. Favorite places for them to locate are between the toes and in the ears although they can appear anywhere on the skin surface.

A good approach to prevent ticks is to remove underbrush and leaf litter, and to thin the trees in areas where dogs are allowed. This removes the cover and food sources for small mammals that serve as hosts for ticks. Ticks must have adequate cover that provides high levels of moisture and at the same time provides an opportunity of contact with animals. Keeping the lawn well maintained also makes ticks less likely to drop by and stay.

Because of the potential for ticks to transmit a variety of harmful diseases, dogs should be carefully inspected after walks through wooded areas (where ticks may be found), and careful removal of all ticks can be very important in the prevention of disease. Care should be taken not to squeeze, crush, or puncture the body of the tick since exposure to body fluids of ticks may lead to spread of any disease carried by that tick to the animal or to the person removing the tick. The tick should be disposed of in a container of alcohol or flushed down the toilet. If the site becomes infected, veterinary attention should be sought immediately. Insecticides and repellents should only be applied to pets following appropriate veterinary advice, since indiscriminate use can be dangerous. Recently, a new tick collar has become available which contains amitraz. This collar not only kills ticks, but causes them to retract from the skin within two to three days. This greatly reduces the chances of ticks transmitting a variety of diseases. A spray formulation has also recently been developed and marketed. It might seem that there should be vaccines for all the diseases carried by ticks, but only a Lyme disease (*Borrelia burgdorferi*) formulation is currently available.

MANGE

Mange refers to any skin condition caused by mites. The contagious mites include ear mites, scabies mites, *Cheyletiella* mites and chiggers. Demodectic mange is associated with proliferation of *Demodex* mites, but they are not considered contagious. Demodicosis is covered in more detail in the chapter on breed-related medical conditions.

The most common causes of mange in dogs are ear mites, and these are extremely contagious. The best way to avoid ear mites is to buy pups from sources that don't have a problem with ear mite infestation. Otherwise, pups readily acquire them when kept in crowded environments in which other animals might be carriers. Treatment is effective if whole body (or systemic) therapy is used, but relapses are common when medication in the ear canal is the only approach. This is because the mites tend to crawl out of the ear canal when medications are instilled. They simply feed elsewhere on the body until it is safe for them to return to the ears.

Scabies mites and *Cheyletiella* mites are passed on by other dogs that are carrying the mites. They are "social" diseases that can be prevented by preventing exposure of your dog to others that are infested. Scabies (sarcoptic mange) has the dubi-

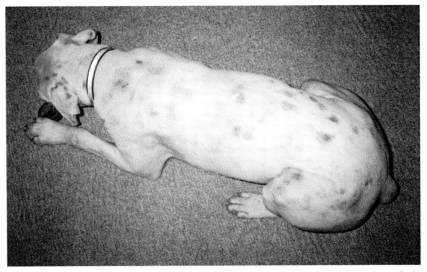

Tashi was underweight and infected with mange (notice the pink patches of skin) when the Michaels family rescued her from an animal shelter.

ous honor of being the most itchy disease to which dogs are susceptible. Chigger mites are present in forested areas and dogs acquire them by roaming in these areas. All can be effectively diagnosed and treated by your veterinarian should your dog happen to become infested.

HEARTWORM

Heartworm disease is caused by the worm *Dirofilaria immitis* and is spread by mosquitoes. The female heartworms produce microfilariae (baby worms) that circulate in the bloodstream, waiting to by picked up by mosquitoes to pass the infection along. Dogs do not get heart-

worm by socializing with infected dogs; they only get infected by mosquitoes that carry the infective microfilariae. The adult heartworms grow in the heart and major blood vessels and eventually cause heart failure.

Fortunately, heartworm is easily prevented by safe oral medications that can be administered daily or on a once-a-month basis. The once-a-month preparations also help prevent many of the common intestinal parasites, such as hookworms, roundworms and whipworms.

Prior to giving any preventative medication for heartworm, an antigen test (an immunologic test that detects heartworms) should be performed by a veterinarian since it is dangerous to give the medication to dogs that harbor the parasite. Some experts also recommend a microfilarial test, just to be doubly certain. Once the test results show that the dog is free of heartworms, the preventative therapy can be commenced. The length of time the heartworm preventatives must be given depends on the length of the mosquito season. In some parts of the country, dogs are on preventative therapy year round. Heartworm vaccines may soon be available but the preventatives now available are easy to administer, inexpensive and quite safe.

Intestinal parasites can cause internal damage, and they pose an especially serious threat to young puppies. Puppies should be dewormed at the earliest possible age.

INTESTINAL PARASITES

The most important internal parasites in dogs are roundworms, hookworms, tapeworms and whipworms. Roundworms are the most common. It has been estimated that 13 trillion roundworm eggs are discharged in dog feces every day! Studies have shown that 75% of all pups carry roundworms and start shedding them by three weeks of age. People are infected by exposure to dog feces containing infective roundworm eggs, not by handling pups. Hookworms can cause a disorder known as *cutaneous larva migrans* in people. In dogs, they are most dangerous to puppies since they latch onto the intestines and suck blood. They can cause anemia and even death when they are present in large numbers. The most common tapeworm is *Dipylidium caninum,* which is spread by fleas. However, another tapeworm (*Echinococcus multilocularis*) can cause fatal disease in people and can be spread to people from dogs. Whipworms live in the lower part of the intestines. Dogs get whipworms by consuming infective larvae. However, it may be another three months before they start shedding them in their stool, greatly complicating diagnosis. In other words, dogs can be infected by whipworms, but fecal evaluations are usually negative until the dog starts passing those eggs three months after being infected.

Other parasites, such as coccidia, *Cryptosporidium*, *Giardia* and flukes can also cause problems in dogs. The best way to prevent all internal parasite problems is to have pups dewormed according to your veterinarian's recommendations, and to have parasite checks done on a regular basis, at least annually.

VIRAL INFECTIONS

Dogs get viral infections such as distemper, hepatitis, parvovirus and rabies by exposure to infected animals. The key to prevention is controlled exposure to other animals and, of course, vaccination. Today's vaccines are extremely effective and properly vaccinated dogs are at minimal risk for contracting these diseases. However, it is still important to limit exposure to other animals that might be harboring infection. When selecting a facility for boarding or groom-

Boxer puppies love to play—especially with each other! Socialization is important for young puppies, but only after they are properly vaccinated. These bouncy baby Boxers are owned by Rick Tomita.

ing an animal, make sure they limit their clientele to animals that have documented vaccine histories. This is in everyone's best interest. Similarly, make sure your veterinarian has a quarantine area for infected dogs and that animals aren't admitted for surgery, boarding, cheaper to do it this way, but might some vaccine ingredients interfere with others? Some say yes, some say no. Are vaccine schedules designed for convenience or effectiveness? Mostly convenience. Some ingredients may only need to be given every two or more years. Research

Eating, sleeping, being cute...these tiny Boxers are much too busy to worry about their medical care, that's what they depend on you for!

grooming or diagnostic testing without up-to-date vaccinations. By controlling exposure and ensuring vaccination, your pet should be safe from these potentially devastating diseases.

It is beyond the scope of this book to settle all the controversies of vaccination, but they are worth mentioning. Should vaccines be combined in a single injection? It's convenient and is incomplete. Should the dose of the vaccine vary with weight or should a Boxer receive the same dose as a Great Dane or Chihuahua? Good questions, no definitive answers. Finally, should we be using modified-live or inactivated vaccine products? There is no short answer for this debate. Ask your veterinarian and do a lot of reading yourself!

CANINE COUGH

Canine infectious tracheo-bronchitis, also known as canine cough and kennel cough, is a contagious viral/bacterial disease that results in a hacking cough that may persist for many weeks. It is common wherever dogs are kept in close quarters, such as kennels, pet stores, nities you give your dog to contact others, the less the likelihood of getting infected. Vaccination is not foolproof because many different viruses can be involved. Parainfluenza virus is included in most vaccines and is one of the more common viruses known to initiate the condition. *Bordetella bronchiseptica* is the

There is a risk of kennel cough whenever dogs are kept together in close quarters. Vaccination is not a foolproof method of protection; limited exposure to other dogs will help reduce the risk.

grooming parlors, dog shows, training classes, and even veterinary clinics. The condition doesn't respond well to most medications, but eventually clears spontaneously over a course of many weeks. Pneumonia is a possible but uncommon complication.

Prevention is best achieved by limiting exposure and utilizing vaccination. The fewer opportu-bacterium most often associated with tracheobronchitis and a vaccine is now available that needs to be repeated twice yearly for dogs at risk. This vaccine is squirted into the nostrils to help stop the infection before it gets deeper into the respiratory tract. Make sure the vaccination is given several days (preferably two weeks) before exposure to ensure maximum protection.

FIRST AID by Judy Iby, RVT

KNOWING YOUR DOG IN GOOD HEALTH

With some experience, you will learn how to give your dog a physical at home, and consequently will learn to recognize many potential problems. If you can detect a problem early, you can seek timely medical help and thereby decrease your dog's risk of developing a more serious problem.

Facing page: Your pet Boxer is an important part of the family. Learning first-aid techniques will help you help your dog in case of an emergency.

Every pet owner should be able to take his pet's temperature, pulse, respirations, and check the capillary refill time (CRT). Knowing what is normal will alert the pet owner to what is abnormal, and this can be life saving for the sick pet.

TEMPERATURE

The dog's normal temperature is 100.5 to 102.5 degrees Fahrenheit. Take the temperature rectally for at least one minute. Be sure to shake the thermometer down first, and you may find it helpful to lubricate the end. It is easy to take the temperature with the dog in a standing position. Be sure to hold on to the thermometer so that it isn't expelled or sucked in. A dog could have an elevated temperature if he is excited or if he is overheated; however, a high temperature could indicate a medical emergency. On the other hand, if the temperature is below 100 degrees, this could also indicate an emergency.

CAPILLARY REFILL TIME AND GUM COLOR

It is important to know how your dog's gums look when he is healthy, so you will be able to recognize a difference if he is not feeling well. There are a few breeds, among them the Chow

Chow and its relatives, that have black gums and a black tongue. This is normal for them. In general, a healthy dog will have bright pink gums. Pale gums are an indication of shock or anemia and are an emergency. Likewise, any yellowish tint is an indication of a sick dog. To check capillary refill time (CRT) press your thumb against the dog's gum. The gum will blanch out (turn white) but should refill (return to the normal pink color) in one to two seconds. CRT is very important. If the refill time is slow and your dog is acting poorly, you should call your veterinarian immediately.

HEART RATE, PULSE, AND RESPIRATIONS

Heart rate depends on the breed of the dog and his health. Normal heart rates range from about 50 beats per minute in the larger breeds to 130 beats per minute in the smaller breeds. You can take the heart rate by pressing your fingertips on the dog's chest. Count for either 10 or 15 seconds, and then multiply by either 6 or 4 to obtain the rate per minute. A normal pulse is the same as the heart rate and is taken at the femoral artery located on the insides of both rear legs. Respirations should be observed and depending on the

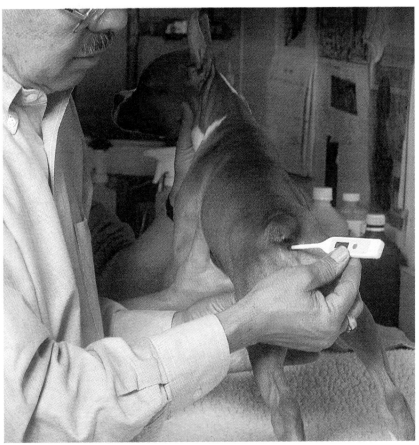

Learn to take your dog's temperature. Anything above or below the normal range of 100.5° F to 102.5° F may be indicative of an emergency.

size and breed of the dog should be 10 to 30 per minute. Obviously, illness or excitement could account for abnormal rates.

PREPARING FOR AN EMERGENCY

It is a good idea to prepare for an emergency by making a list and keeping it by the phone.

This list should include:

1. Your veterinarian's name, address, phone number, and office hours.

2. Your veterinarian's policy for after-hour care. Does he take his own emergencies or does he refer them to an emergency clinic?

3. The name, address, phone

number and hours of the emergency clinic your veterinarian uses.

4. The number of the National Poison Control Center for Animals in Illinois: 1-800-548-2423. It is open 24 hours a day.

In a true emergency, time is of the essence. Some signs of an emergency may be:

1. Pale gums or an abnormal heart rate.
2. Abnormal temperature, lower than 100 degrees or over 104 degrees.
3. Shock or lethargy.
4. Spinal paralysis.

A dog hit by a car needs to be checked out and probably should have radiographs of the chest and abdomen to rule out pneumothorax or ruptured bladder.

EMERGENCY MUZZLE

An injured, frightened dog may not even recognize his owner and may be inclined to bite. If your dog should be injured, you may need to muzzle him to protect yourself before you try to handle him. It is a good idea to practice muzzling the calm, healthy dog so you understand the technique. Slip a lead over his head for control. You can tie his mouth shut with something like a two-foot-long

bandage or piece of cloth. A necktie, stocking, leash or even a piece of rope will also work.

1. Make a large loop by tying a loose knot in the middle of the bandage or cloth.
2. Hold the ends up, one in each hand.
3. Slip the loop over the dog's muzzle and lower jaw, just behind his nose.
4. Quickly tighten the loop so he can't open his mouth.
5. Tie the ends under his lower jaw.
6. Make a knot there and pull the ends back on each side of his face, under the ears, to the back of his head.

If he should start to vomit, you will need to remove the muzzle immediately. Otherwise, he could aspirate vomitus into his lungs.

ANTIFREEZE POISONING

Antifreeze in the driveway is a potential killer. Because antifreeze is sweet, dogs will lap it up. The active ingredient in antifreeze is ethylene glycol, which causes irreversible kidney damage. If you witness your pet ingesting antifreeze, you should call your veterinarian immediately. He may recommend that you induce vomiting at once by using hydrogen peroxide, or he may recommend a test to confirm antifreeze ingestion. Treatment is aggressive and must be administered promptly if the dog is to live, but you wouldn't want to subject your dog to unnecessary treatment.

BEE STINGS

A severe reaction to a bee sting (anaphylaxis) can result in difficulty breathing, collapse and even death. A symptom of a bee sting is swelling around the muzzle and face. Bee stings are antihistamine responsive. It is safest and most effective to contact your veterinarian for recommendations on safe antihistamines and the doses to administer. You should monitor the dog's gum color and respirations and watch for a decrease in swelling. If your dog is showing signs of anaphylaxis, your veterinarian may need to give him an injection of corticosteroids. It would be wise to call your veterinarian and confirm treatment.

BLEEDING

Bleeding can occur in many forms, such as a ripped dewclaw, a toenail cut too short, a puncture wound, a severe laceration, etc. If a pressure bandage is needed, it must be re-

Anemia, as evidenced by pale gums. Pale gums can also indicate other emergency situations, such as a severe reaction to a bee sting. Courtesy of Dr. Kenneth Jeffery.

leased every 15–20 minutes. Be careful of elastic bandages since it is easy to apply them too tightly. Any bandage material should be clean. If no regular bandage is available, a small towel or wash cloth can be used to cover the wound and bind it with a necktie, scarf, or something similar. Styptic powder, or even a soft cake of soap, can be used to stop a bleeding toenail. A ripped dewclaw or toenail may need to be cut back by the veterinarian and possibly treated with antibiotics. Depending on their severity, lacerations and puncture wounds may also need professional treatment. Your first thought should be to clean the wound with peroxide, soap and water, or some other antiseptic cleanser. Don't use alcohol since it deters the healing of the tissue.

BLOAT

Although not generally considered a first aid situation, bloat can occur in a dog rather suddenly. Truly, it is an emergency! Gastric dilatation-volvulus or gastric torsion—the twisting of the stomach to cut off both entry and exit, causing the organ to "bloat," is a disorder primarily found in the larger, more deepchested breeds. It is life threatening and requires immediate veterinary assistance.

BURNS

If your dog gets a chemical burn, call your veterinarian immediately. Rinse any other burns with cold water and if the burn is significant, call your veterinarian. It may be necessary to clip the hair around the burn so it will be easier to keep clean. You can cleanse the wound on a daily basis with saline and apply a topical antimicrobial ointment, such as silver sulfadiazine 1 percent cream or gentamicin cream. Burns can be debilitating, especially to an older pet. They can cause pain and shock. It takes about three weeks for the skin to slough after the burn and there is the possibility of permanent hair loss.

CARDIOPULMONARY RESUSCITATION (CPR)

Check to see if your dog has a heart beat, pulse and spontaneous respiration. If his pupils are already dilated and fixed, the prognosis is less favorable. This is an emergency situation that requires two people to administer lifesaving techniques. One person needs to breathe for the dog while the other person tries to establish heart rhythm. Mouth to mouth resuscitation starts with two initial breaths, one to one and a half seconds in duration. After the initial breaths, breathe for the dog once after every five chest compressions. (You do not want to expand the dog's lungs while his chest is being compressed.) You inhale, cover the dog's nose with your mouth, and exhale *gently*. You should see the dog's chest expand. Sometimes, pulling the tongue forward stimulates respiration. You should be ventilating the dog 12–20 times per minute. The person managing the chest compressions should have the dog lying on his right side with one hand on either side of the dog's chest, directed over the heart between the fourth and fifth ribs (usually this is the point of the flexed elbow). The number of compressions administered depends on the size of the patient. Attempt 80–120 compressions per minute. Check for spontaneous respiration and/or heart beat. If present, monitor the patient and discontinue resuscitation. If you haven't already done so, call your veterinarian at once and make arrangements to take your pet in for professional treatment.

CHOCOLATE TOXICOSIS

Dogs like chocolate, but chocolate kills dogs. Its two basic chemicals, caffeine and theobromine, overstimulate the dog's nervous system. Ten ounces of milk choco-

Puppies need to chew— therefore, they need safe things to chew on. Nylabone® chew products are made of durable nylon and are recommended by veterinarians around the world.

late can kill a 12-pound dog. Symptoms of poisoning include restlessness, vomiting, increased heart rate, seizure, and coma. Death is possible. If your dog has ingested chocolate, you can give syrup of ipecac at a dosage of one-eighth of a teaspoon per pound to induce vomiting. Two tablespoons of hydrogen peroxide is an alternative treatment.

CHOKING

You need to open the dog's mouth to see if any object is visible. Try to hold him upside down to see if the object can be dislodged. While you are working on your dog, call your veterinarian, as time may be critical.

DOG BITES

If your dog is bitten, wash the area and determine the severity of the situation. Some bites may need immediate attention, for instance, if it is bleeding profusely or if a lung is punctured. Other bites may be only superficial scrapes. Most dog bite cases need to be seen by the veterinarian, and some may require antibiotics. It is important that you learn if the offending dog has had a rabies vaccination. This is important for your dog, but also for you, in case you are the victim. Wash the wound and call your doctor for further instructions. You should check on your tetanus vaccination history. Rarely, and I mean rarely, do dogs get tetanus. If the offending dog is a stray, try to confine him for observation. He will need to be confined for ten days. A dog that has bitten a human and is not current on his rabies vaccination cannot receive a rabies vaccination for ten days. Dog bites should be reported to the Board of Health.

DROWNING

Remove any debris from the dog's mouth and swing the dog, holding him upside down. Stimulate respiration by pulling his tongue forward. Administer CPR if necessary, and call your veterinarian. Don't give up working on the dog. Be sure to wrap him in blankets if he is cold or in shock.

ELECTROCUTION

You may want to look into puppy proofing your house by installing GFCIs (Ground Fault Circuit Interrupters) on your electrical outlets. A GFCI just saved my dog's life. He had pulled an extension cord into his crate and was "teething" on it at seven years of age. The GFCI kept him from being electrocuted. Turn off the current before touching the dog. Resuscitate him by administering CPR and pulling his tongue forward to stimulate respiration. Try mouth-to-mouth breathing if the dog is not breathing. Take him to your veterinarian as soon as possible since electrocution can cause internal problems, such as lung damage, which need medical treatment.

EYES

Red eyes indicate inflammation, and any redness to the upper white part of the eye (sclera) may constitute an emergency. Squinting, cloudiness to the cornea, or loss of vision could indicate severe problems, such as glaucoma, anterior uveitis and episcleritis. Glaucoma is an emergency if you want to save the dog's eye. A prolapsed third eyelid is abnormal and is a symptom of an underlying problem. If something should get in your dog's eye, flush it out with cold water or a saline eye wash. Epiphora and allergic conjunctivitis are annoying and frequently persistent problems. Epiphora (excessive tearing) leaves the area below the eye wet and sometimes stained. The wetness may lead to a bacterial infection. There are numerous causes (allergies, infections, foreign matter, abnormally located eyelashes and adjacent facial hair that rubs against the eyeball, defects or diseases of the tear drainage system, birth defects of the eyelids, etc.) and the treatment is based on the cause. Keeping the hair around the eye cut short and sponging the eye daily will give relief. Many cases are responsive to medical treatment. Allergic conjunctivitis may be a seasonal problem if the dog has inhalant allergies (e.g., ragweed), or it may be a year 'round problem. The conjunctiva becomes red and swollen and is prone to a bacterial infection associated with mucus accumulation or pus in the eye. Again keeping the hair around the eyes short will give relief. Mild corticosteroid drops or ointment will also give relief.

The underlying problem should be investigated.

FISH HOOKS

An imbedded fish hook will probably need to be removed by the veterinarian. More than likely, sedation will be required along with antibiotics. Don't try to remove it yourself. The shank of the hook will need to be cut off in order to push the other end through.

FOREIGN OBJECTS

I can't tell you how many chicken bones my first dog ingested. Fortunately she had a "cast iron stomach" and never suffered the consequences. However, she was always going to the veterinarian for treatment. Not all dogs are so lucky. It is unbelievable what some dogs will take a liking to. I have assisted in surgeries in which all kinds of foreign objects were removed from the stomach and/or intestinal tract. Those objects included socks, pantyhose, stockings, clothing, diapers, sanitary products, plastic, toys, and, last but not least, rawhides. Surgery is costly and not always successful, especially if it is performed too late. If you see or suspect your dog has ingested a foreign object, contact your veterinarian immediately. He may tell you to induce vomiting or he may have you bring your dog to the clinic immediately. Don't induce vomiting without the veterinarian's permission, since the object may cause more damage on the way back up than it would if you allow it to pass through.

HEATSTROKE

Heatstroke is an emergency! The classic signs are rapid, shallow breathing; rapid heartbeat; a temperature above 104 degrees; and subsequent collapse. The dog needs to be cooled as quickly as possible and treated immediately by the veterinarian. If possible, spray him down with cool water and pack ice around his head, neck, and groin. Monitor his temperature and stop the cooling process as soon as his temperature reaches 103 degrees. Nevertheless, you will need to keep monitoring his temperature to be sure it doesn't elevate again. If the temperature continues to drop to below 100 degrees, it could be life threatening. Get professional help immediately. Prevention is more successful than treatment. Those at the greatest risk are brachycephalic (short nosed) breeds, obese dogs, and those that suffer from cardiovascular disease. Dogs are not able to cool off by sweating as people can. Their only way is through panting and radiation of heat from the skin surface. When stressed and exposed to high environmental temperature, high humidity, and poor ventilation, a dog can suffer heatstroke very quickly. Many people do not realize how quickly a car can overheat. Never leave a dog unattended in a car. It is even against the law in some states. Also, a brachycephalic, obese, or infirm dog should never be left unattended outside during inclement weather and should have his activities curtailed. Any dog left outside, by law, must be assured adequate shelter (including shade) and fresh water.

POISONS

Try to locate the source of the poison (the container which lists the ingredients) and call your veterinarian immediately. Be prepared to give the age and weight of your dog, the quantity of poison consumed and the probable time of ingestion. Your veterinarian will want you to read off the ingredients. If you can't reach him, you can call a local poison center or the National Poison Control Center for Animals in Illinois, which is open 24 hours a day. Their phone number is 1-800-548-2423. There is a charge for their service, so you may need to have a credit card number available.

Symptoms of poisoning include muscle trembling and weakness, increased salivation, vomiting and loss of bowel control. There are numerous household toxins (over 500,000). A up to the kitchen counters, but when I owned a large breed she would clean the counter, eating all the prescription medications.

Your pet can be poisoned by means other than directly in-

A stream may look inviting to a thirsty Boxer, but you never know what toxins or bacteria the water contains. It's safer to bring along clean water for your dog when exploring the great outdoors.

dog can be poisoned by toxins in the garbage. Other poisons include pesticides, pain relievers, prescription drugs, plants, chocolate, and cleansers. Since I own small dogs I don't have to worry about my dogs jumping gesting the toxin. Ingesting a rodent that has ingested a rodenticide is one example. It is possible for a dog to have a reaction to the pesticides used by exterminators. If this is suspected you should contact the exterminator about the potential dangers of the pesticides used and their side effects.

Don't give human drugs to your dog unless your veterinarian has given his approval. Some human medications can be deadly to dogs.

POISONOUS PLANTS

Amaryllis (bulb)	Jasmine (berries)
Andromeda	Jerusalem Cherry
Apple Seeds (cyanide)	Jimson Weed
Arrowgrass	Laburnum
Avocado	Larkspur
Azalea	Laurel
Bittersweet	Locoweed
Boxwood	Marigold
Buttercup	Marijuana
Caladium	Mistletoe (berries)
Castor Bean	Monkshood
Cherry Pits	Mushrooms
Chokecherry	Narcissus (bulb)
Climbing Lily	Nightshade
Crown of Thorns	Oleander
Daffodil (bulb)	Peach
Daphne	Philodendron
Delphinium	Poison Ivy
Dieffenbachia	Privet
Dumb Cane	Rhododendron
Elderberry	Rhubarb
Elephant Ear	Snow on
English Ivy	the Mountain
Foxglove	Stinging Nettle
Hemlock	Toadstool
Holly	Tobacco
Hyacinth (bulb)	Tulip (bulb)
Hydrangea	Walnut
Iris (bulb)	Wisteria
Japanese Yew	Yew

This list was published in the American Kennel Club *Gazette*, February, 1995. As the list states these are common poisonous plants, but this list may not be complete. If your dog ingests a poisonous plant, try to identify it and call your veterinarian. Some plants cause more harm than others.

PORCUPINE QUILLS

Removal of quills is best left up to your veterinarian since it can be quite painful. Your unhappy dog would probably appreciate being sedated for the removal of the quills.

SEIZURE (CONVULSION OR FIT)

Many breeds, including mixed breeds, are predisposed to seizures, although a seizure may be secondary to an underlying medical condition. Usually a seizure is not considered an emergency unless it lasts longer than ten minutes. Nevertheless, you should notify your veterinarian. Dogs do not swallow their tongues. Do not handle the dog's mouth since your dog probably cannot control his actions and may inadvertently bite you. The seizure can be mild; for instance, a dog can have a seizure standing up. More frequently the dog will lose consciousness and may urinate and/or defecate. The best thing you can do for your dog is to put him in a safe place or to block off the stairs or areas where he can fall.

SEVERE TRAUMA

See that the dog's head and neck are extended so if the dog is unconscious or in shock, he is able to breathe. If there is any vomitus, you should try to get the head extended down with the body elevated to prevent vomitus from being aspirated. Alert your veterinarian that you are on your way.

SHOCK

Shock is a life threatening condition and requires immediate veterinary care. It can occur after an injury or even after severe fright. Other causes of shock are hemorrhage, fluid loss, sepsis, toxins, adrenal insufficiency, cardiac failure, and anaphylaxis. The symptoms are a rapid weak pulse, shallow breathing, dilated pupils, subnormal temperature, and muscle weakness. The capillary refill time (CRT) is slow, taking longer than two seconds for normal gum color to return. Keep the dog warm while transporting him to the veterinary clinic. Time is critical for survival.

SKUNKS

Skunk spraying is not necessarily an emergency, although it would be in my house. If the dog's eyes are sprayed, you need to rinse them well with water. One remedy for deskunking the dog is to wash him in tomato juice and follow with a soap and water bath. The newest remedy is bathing the dog in a mixture

of one quart of three percent hydrogen peroxide, quarter cup baking soda, and one teaspoon liquid soap. Rinse well. There are also commercial products available.

SNAKE BITES

It is always a good idea to know what poisonous snakes reside in your area. Rattlesnakes, water moccasins, copperheads, and coral snakes are residents of some areas of the United States.

A healthy Boxer is a sociable Boxer! This outgoing pup waves hello to a friend. Owned by Steven G. and Ann B. Anderson.

Pack ice around the area that is bitten and call your veterinarian immediately to alert him that you are on your way. Try to identify the snake or at least be able to describe it (for the use of antivenin). It is possible that he may send you to another clinic that has the proper antivenin.

It's natural for an inquisitive puppy to want to explore, but who knows what nasty surprises he may encounter in the tall grass?

TOAD POISONING

Bufo toads are quite deadly. You should find out if these nasty little critters are native to your area.

VACCINATION REACTION

Once in a while, a dog may suffer an anaphylactic reaction to a vaccine. Symptoms include swelling around the muzzle, extending to the eyes. Your veterinarian may ask you to return to his office to determine the severity of the reaction. It is possible that your dog may need to stay at the hospital for a few hours during future vaccinations.

RECOMMENDED READING

DR. ACKERMAN'S DOG BOOKS FROM T.F.H.

OWNER'S GUIDE TO DOG HEALTH

TS-214, 432 pages
Over 300 color photographs

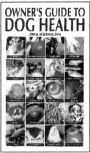

Winner of the 1995 Dog Writers Association of America's Best Health Book, this comprehensive title gives accurate, up-to-date information on all the major disorders and conditions found in dogs. Completely illustrated to help owners visualize signs of illness, different states of infection, procedures and treatment, it covers nutrition, skin disorders, disorders of the major body systems (reproductive, digestive, respiratory), eye problems, vaccines and vaccinations, dental health and more.

SKIN & COAT CARE FOR YOUR DOG

TS-249 224 pages
Over 200 color photographs

Dr. Ackerman, a specialist in the field of dermatology and a Diplomate of the American College of Veterinary Dermatology, joins 14 of the world's most respected dermatologists and other experts to produce an extremely helpful manual on the dog's skin. Coat and skin problems are extremely common in the dog, and owners need to better understand the conditions that affect their dogs' coats. The book details everything from the basics of parasites and mange to grooming techniques, medications, hair loss and more.

DOG BEHAVIOR AND TRAINING
Veterinary Advice for Owners

TS-252, 292 pages
Over 200 color photographs

Joined by co-editors Gary Landsberg, DVM and Wayne Hunthausen, DVM, Dr. Ackerman and about 20 experts in behavioral studies and training set forth a practical guide to the common problems owners experience with their dogs. Since behavioral disorders are the number-one reason for owners to abandon a dog, it is essential for owners to understand how the dog thinks and how to correct him if he misbehaves. The book covers socialization, selection, rewards and punishment, puppy-problem prevention, excitable and disobedient behaviors, sexual behaviors, aggression, children, stress and more.

RECOMMENDED READING

BOXER BOOKS FROM T.F.H.

THE BOXER
by Anna Katherine Nicholas
PS-813, 256 pages
Over 100 photos

Written by internationally known and respected dog show judge and author Anna Katherine Nicholas, *The Boxer* is a wonderful reference for the serious show exhibitor and the dedicated pet owner alike. Full color and black-and-white photographs bring the pages to life. Topics discussed include: breed history in various parts of the world, the breed standard, the Boxer's characteristics and special talents, caring for a Boxer, showing your Boxer, responsibilities of breeders and owners, and much more.

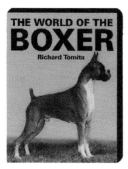

THE WORLD OF THE BOXER
by Rick Tomita
TS-273,
Over 1000 photos

Richard Tomita has assembled the most complete volume on the Boxer breed ever to be published. *The World of the Boxer* presents hundreds of the most important and influential Boxers, the kennels that produced them, and a comprehensive overview of the Boxer breed around the world. In addition to complete chapters on the United States, Australia, Canada and England, the author discusses Boxers in Germany and the Continent, as well as Japan, Brazil, India, Mexico, South Africa, and elsewhere. Chapters include showing and training the Boxer, history of the American Boxer Club, genetics, obedience, judging, and a special chapter on breeding, whelping and puppy care written only as this expert breeder can do. No Boxer lover will do without this breed book masterpiece, an absolute essential for every Boxer library.

A NEW OWNER'S GUIDE TO BOXERS
by Rick Tomita
JG-103, 160 pages
Over 150 full color photos

The world's number-one Boxer breeder shares his 25 years of experience in this comprehensive volume that covers everything the responsible dog owner needs to know. A brief breed history is discussed, as well as the breed standard, selecting and caring for your puppy, training and showing your dog, and health and dental care. Learn about the Boxer's talents and roles in today's society, and how to understand your dog's behavior and how he communicates.